THE
BODY
ATLAS

By Steve Parker
Illustrated by Giuliano Fornari

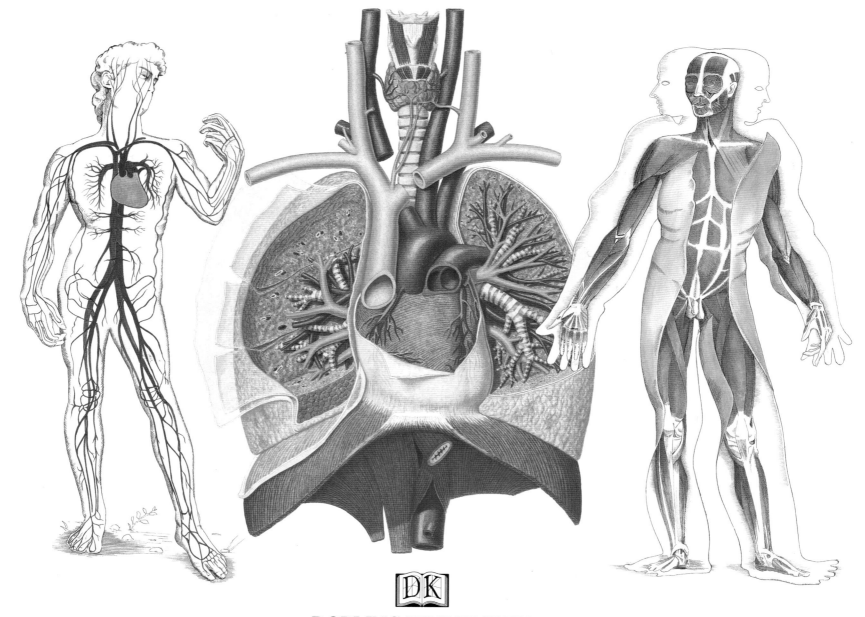

DK

DORLING KINDERSLEY
LONDON · NEW YORK · STUTTGART

DK

A DORLING KINDERSLEY BOOK

Senior Art Editor Christopher Gillingwater

Project Editors Laura L. Buller and Constance Novis

U.S. Editor B. Alison Weir

Designer Dorian Spencer Davies

Production Neil Palfreyman and Marguerite Fenn

Managing Editor Susan Peach

Managing Art Editor Jacquie Gulliver

Consultants Dr. Thomas Kramer MBBS, MRCS, LRCP and

Thaddeus M. Yablonsky, M.D.

First American Edition, 1993
2 4 6 8 10 9 7 5 3 1

Published in the United States by
Dorling Kindersley, Inc., 232 Madison Avenue
New York, New York 10016

Library of Congress Cataloging–in–Publication Data

Parker, Steve.
  The body atlas / by Steve Parker ; illustrated by Giuliano Fornari. —1st American ed.
  p. : ill. ; cm.
  Includes index.
  ISBN 1-56458-224-8
  1. Human anatomy—Atlases—Juvenile literature. I. Fornari, Giuliano. II. Title.
QM27.P266 1993
611—dc20   92-54307
                                                        CIP
                                                        AC

Reproduced in Essex by Dot Gradations
Printed and bound in Italy by New Interlitho, Milan

Contents

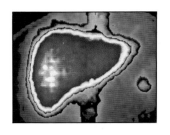
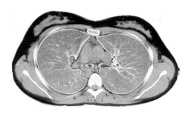

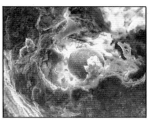
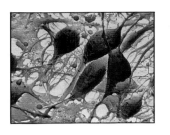

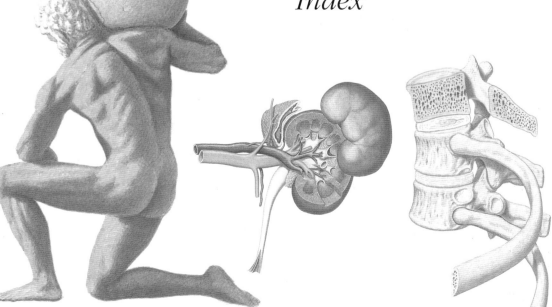

Mapping the Human Body

THIS BOOK INTRODUCES the exciting world inside you – the world of the human body. The drawings on the following pages map one body, exploring it from head to toe, one major region at a time. The artwork reveals what goes on inside each of these regions, giving you a closer look at the vital structures within. You will see how each organ works individually, and find out how it interacts with the body parts around it.

Your body may not look exactly like the body mapped here. Where there are differences – as there are between the female and male sexes, for example – separate pictures show you what these differences are. There are also variations in height, weight, skin and hair color, bone proportions, and other features, that make each of us an individual within the human species *Homo sapiens*.

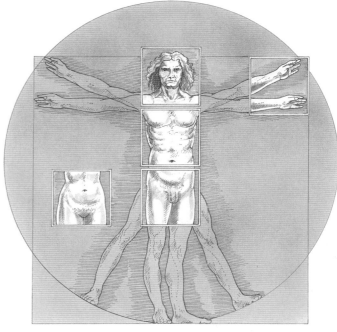

THE OUTSIDES OF YOUR INSIDES

The Body Atlas shows what your body parts look like from the outside and the inside – even from the front and back. Some body parts are shown in realistic form and color, as in this view of the outside of the heart, its wrappings, and the major blood vessels surrounding it.

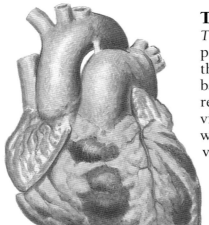

INSIDE YOUR INSIDES

Body parts are also shown with the outsides peeled back, and sometimes removed, to reveal the insides. This view, for example, shows the inner chambers, linings, valves, and muscles of the heart. Arteries, veins, and nerves are shown in three different colors, making them easy to identify.

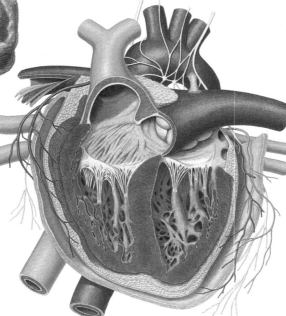

IMAGES FROM LIFE

Photographs in *The Body Atlas* use the latest imaging techniques, allowing you to examine parts you could never see with your eyes. Computer-enhanced, color-coded X-rays, such as the one on the right, reveal the intricate forms of bones and organs under the skin. Below is a photograph taken with a scanning electron microscope. It displays structures as small as an individual cell.

A photomicrograph (a photograph taken with a microscope) of a glomerulus, the ball of tiny capillaries inside the kidney

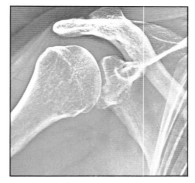

An X-ray of the bones in the shoulder joint, showing how the rounded end of the upper-arm bone fits into a cup-shaped socket in the shoulder blade

FINDING YOUR WAY

The Body Atlas is divided into sections that deal with the major regions of the body, such as the head and neck, the upper torso, or the arm and hand. Each section is identified next to the main page title by an illustration of that region, as shown above. Like the outlines of continents in a world atlas, these illustrations provide a quick guide to the region's location in the body – no matter how unfamiliar the "landscape."

LAYER BY LAYER

This book lifts away each layer of the body, so that you can see how the structures inside fit and work with those around them. Under the skin, muscle layers, and front bones are the main organs, such as the brain, lungs, heart, liver, stomach, and intestines. Blood vessels and nerves snake between these, and out into the limbs. Deeper still are more skeletal bones, which provide a firm framework for support and movement. Behind them are more muscles and vessels, and another layer of fat and skin.

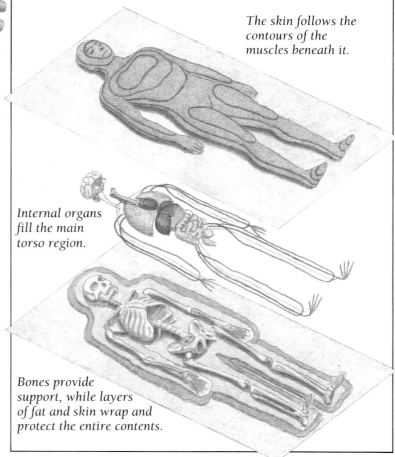

The skin follows the contours of the muscles beneath it.

Internal organs fill the main torso region.

Bones provide support, while layers of fat and skin wrap and protect the entire contents.

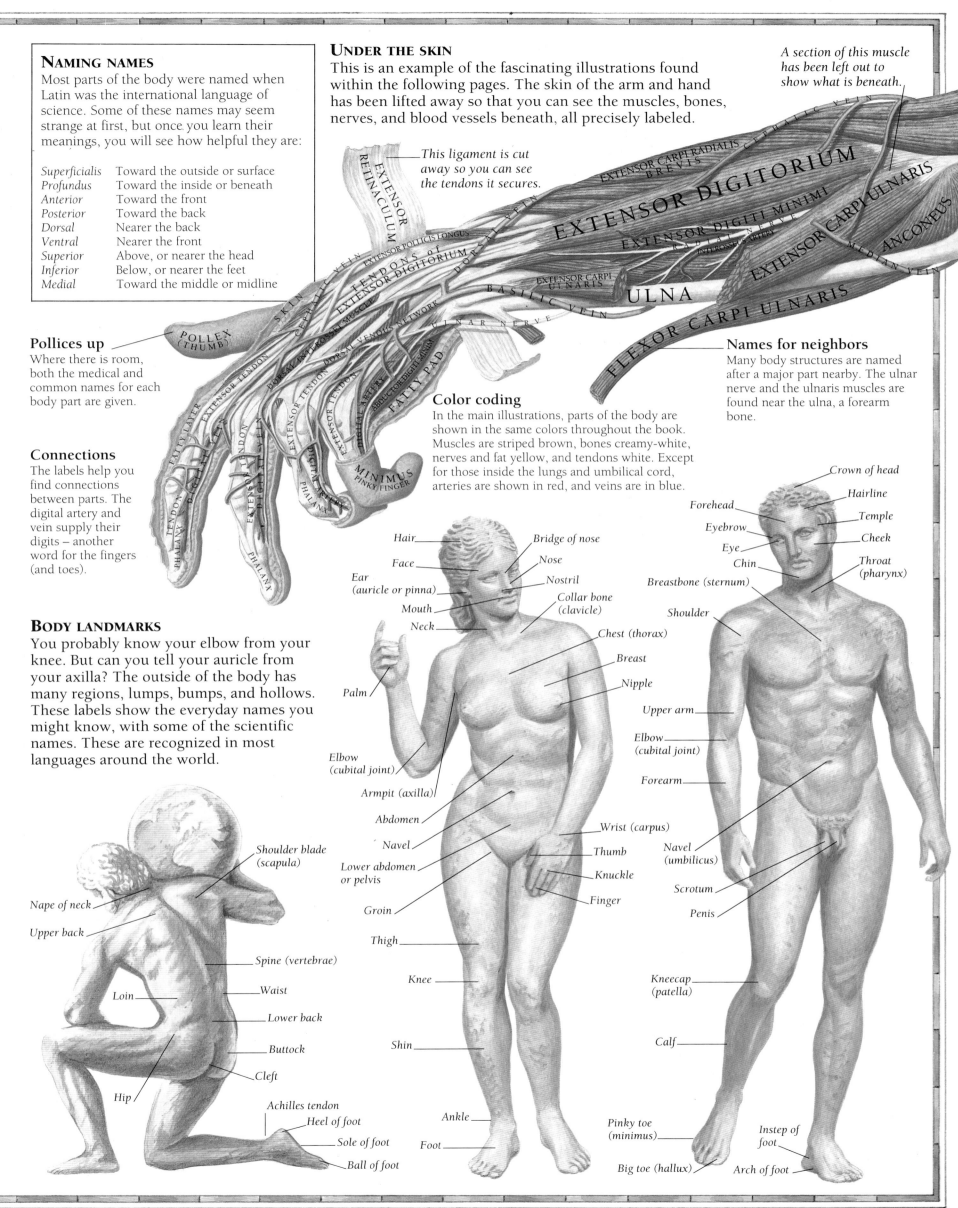

NAMING NAMES

Most parts of the body were named when Latin was the international language of science. Some of these names may seem strange at first, but once you learn their meanings, you will see how helpful they are:

Superficialis	Toward the outside or surface
Profundus	Toward the inside or beneath
Anterior	Toward the front
Posterior	Toward the back
Dorsal	Nearer the back
Ventral	Nearer the front
Superior	Above, or nearer the head
Inferior	Below, or nearer the feet
Medial	Toward the middle or midline

UNDER THE SKIN

This is an example of the fascinating illustrations found within the following pages. The skin of the arm and hand has been lifted away so that you can see the muscles, bones, nerves, and blood vessels beneath, all precisely labeled.

A section of this muscle has been left out to show what is beneath.

This ligament is cut away so you can see the tendons it secures.

Pollices up

Where there is room, both the medical and common names for each body part are given.

Connections

The labels help you find connections between parts. The digital artery and vein supply their digits – another word for the fingers (and toes).

Names for neighbors

Many body structures are named after a major part nearby. The ulnar nerve and the ulnaris muscles are found near the ulna, a forearm bone.

Color coding

In the main illustrations, parts of the body are shown in the same colors throughout the book. Muscles are striped brown, bones creamy-white, nerves and fat yellow, and tendons white. Except for those inside the lungs and umbilical cord, arteries are shown in red, and veins are in blue.

BODY LANDMARKS

You probably know your elbow from your knee. But can you tell your auricle from your axilla? The outside of the body has many regions, lumps, bumps, and hollows. These labels show the everyday names you might know, with some of the scientific names. These are recognized in most languages around the world.

Arm illustration labels: EXTENSOR RETINACULUM, EXTENSOR POLLICIS LONGUS, TENDONS of EXTENSOR DIGITORIUM MUSCLE, SKIN LAYER, CEPHALIC VEIN, DORSAL VEIN, DORSAL INTEROSSEOUS MUSCLE, DORSAL VENOUS NETWORK, ULNAR NERVE, EXTENSOR CARPI ULNARIS, BASILIC VEIN, ULNA, EXTENSOR CARPI RADIALIS BREVIS, EXTENSOR DIGITORIUM, EXTENSOR DIGITI MINIMI, RADIAL NERVE, INTEROSSEOUS ARTERY, CEPHALIC VEIN, ANCONEUS, MEDIAN VEIN, EXTENSOR CARPI ULNARIS, FLEXOR CARPI ULNARIS, POLLEX (THUMB), FATTY LAYER, EXTENSOR TENDON, DIGITAL VEIN, EXTENSOR TENDON, DIGITAL VEIN, EXTENSOR TENDON, DIGITAL ARTERY, EXTENSOR TENDON, DIGITAL ARTERY, ABDUCTOR DIGITI MINIMI, FATTY PAD, MINIMUS PINKY FINGER, PHALANX

Back/kneeling figure labels: Nape of neck, Upper back, Shoulder blade (scapula), Loin, Spine (vertebrae), Waist, Lower back, Buttock, Cleft, Hip, Achilles tendon, Heel of foot, Sole of foot, Ball of foot

Female figure labels: Hair, Face, Ear (auricle or pinna), Mouth, Neck, Palm, Elbow (cubital joint), Armpit (axilla), Abdomen, Navel, Lower abdomen or pelvis, Groin, Thigh, Knee, Shin, Ankle, Foot, Bridge of nose, Nose, Nostril, Collar bone (clavicle), Chest (thorax), Breast, Nipple, Wrist (carpus), Thumb, Knuckle, Finger

Male figure labels: Crown of head, Forehead, Eyebrow, Eye, Chin, Breastbone (sternum), Shoulder, Hairline, Temple, Cheek, Throat (pharynx), Upper arm, Elbow (cubital joint), Forearm, Navel (umbilicus), Scrotum, Penis, Kneecap (patella), Calf, Pinky toe (minimus), Big toe (hallux), Instep of foot, Arch of foot

Support and Movement

THE BILLIONS OF CELLS inside your body link to form tissues, special cell groups with one main job to do. Groups of one or more kinds of tissues make up your body's main parts, the organs. A collection of organs that work together to fulfill a major function is called a body system. You are reading this book, for example, using your eyes, an important part of your sensory system. They are scanning the illustrations and words and, in an instant, reporting the information to your brain, the central organ of your nervous system. At the same time, other body systems are carrying out the tasks that keep you alive. Your heart and blood vessels form your circulatory system, which carries blood around your body, and your lungs are the main part of your respiratory system, which breathes in air.

Although each of the systems has a distinct function, none is by any means independent from the others. Each relies on other systems, working with them so that your whole body functions smoothly and efficiently.

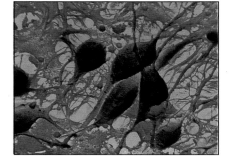

These are nerve cells, which group to form the tissue that makes up the organs of the nervous system.

THE BODY'S MAIN SYSTEMS

Your major body systems are shown on the next four pages. In some systems, the parts are grouped together. For example, the organs of the digestive system are packed into your abdomen. In other systems, the parts are spread throughout your body, such as the blood vessels of your circulatory system.

INSIDE A CELL

Cells are your body's microscopic building blocks. You have more than 50 billion of them, forming your bones, muscles, nerves, skin, blood, and other organs and body tissues. The drawing below shows a "typical" cell, cut away to expose the even smaller parts, called organelles, inside it. Cells similar in shape to the one shown here exist only in a few parts of the body, such as the liver. In most other parts, the cells are of different sizes and shapes, specialized to do particular jobs – like the nerve cells above, the fat cell opposite, and the blood cells on page 8.

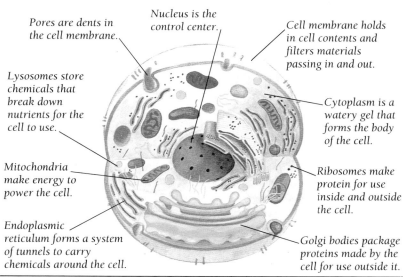

Pores are dents in the cell membrane.

Nucleus is the control center.

Cell membrane holds in cell contents and filters materials passing in and out.

Lysosomes store chemicals that break down nutrients for the cell to use.

Cytoplasm is a watery gel that forms the body of the cell.

Mitochondria make energy to power the cell.

Ribosomes make protein for use inside and outside the cell.

Endoplasmic reticulum forms a system of tunnels to carry chemicals around the cell.

Golgi bodies package proteins made by the cell for use outside it.

SKELETAL SYSTEM

From the top of your head to the tips of your toes, bones play a vital supporting role for the softer parts of your body. Your skeleton consists of 206 individual bones, linked to each other at joints. They provide a strong yet flexible framework that is moved by your muscles. Some bones surround and protect more delicate organs, such as the skull around your brain and the ribs encasing your heart and lungs.

Mandible (lower jaw)

Cervical (neck) vertebrae

Scapula (shoulder blade)

Elbow joint

Wrist joint

Skull
The 28 bones in your skull and face make a box for your brain, eyes, and ears.

Rib cage
Protecting your heart and lungs are the 24 curved bones of the rib cage.

Humerus
The long bone between your shoulder and elbow joints is the humerus.

Radius and ulna
The radius, on the thumb side of the arm, and the ulna swivel over each other when you twist your wrist.

Carpals (wrist bones)

Metacarpals (palm bones)

Phalanges (finger bones)

Sacrum

Pelvis
The bowl shape of the pelvis cradles the organs in your lower abdomen.

Patella
The kneecap, or patella, is an unusual bone. It is not joined directly to another bone; instead, it is embedded in the straplike tendon of the knee joint.

Tarsals (ankle bones)

Metatarsals (sole bones)

Phalanges (toe bones)

Long and strong
The femur, or thigh bone, is the longest bone in your body, and one of the strongest. It helps support your weight when you stand.

Tibia and fibula
Anchoring your powerful lower leg muscles are two bones, the thicker tibia, or shin bone, and its slimmer partner, the fibula, or calf bone.

Foot bones
The 26 bones in your foot make an arch strong enough to support your body when you stand up, and flexible enough to spring back into shape when you sit down.

MUSCULAR SYSTEM

There are more than 650 individual muscles in your body, providing pulling power so that you can move around. Most are attached to bones or to other muscles by tough cords called tendons. In addition, many body organs, such as the heart, intestines, and bladder, contain their own muscle. Unlike bones, which often have everyday names, most muscles are known only by their scientific names. These often twist the most flexible muscle of all - your tongue!

INTEGUMENTARY SYSTEM

This is the scientific name for the skin, hair, nails, and glands covering your body. The surface of the skin consists of dead, hardened cells like tiles on a roof, which are rubbed off as you move, wear clothes, and wash. Yet just below its surface, your skin is very much alive, and very busy. Its cells multiply every second to replace those worn away.

A fat, or adipose, cell contains "blobs" of fat that can be used for energy when food is scarce.

Extensor muscles of hand

Temporalis
Anchored at the temple, this muscle helps you clench your teeth.

Triceps
"Tri" means three. The triceps attaches to the bone beneath it at three points.

Splenius capitis

Melanin
Pigment cells called melanocytes give your skin, hair, and eyes their color.

The skin of your lips is thin and sensitive.

Fat layer
Underneath the skin, a layer of fat insulates your body and helps its temperature stay steady.

EXTENSOR MUSCLE
EXTENSOR MUSCLE
EXTENSOR

DELTOID
TRAPEZIUS
TRAPEZIUS
TERES
TERES
DELTOID
BICEPS
TRICEPS
TRICEPS

LATISSIMUS DORSI

Bulging biceps
If you bend your elbow and clench your fist, you might see a bulge in this muscle.

Breathe out
The external oblique muscle wraps around your ribs and helps you exhale.

Fascia
This stretchy tissue separates muscle groups.

Keep cool
Your skin contains sweat glands to help keep you cool on hot days.

DELTOID
PECTORALIS
PECTORALIS MAJOR
BICEPS
BICEPS
FLEXOR MUSCLE
FLEXOR MUSCLE
EXTENSOR MUSCLE
FLEXOR
EXTENSOR

RECTUS ABDOMINIS

FLEXOR MUSCLE

FASCIA OF BACK

EXTERNAL OBLIQUE

GLUTEUS MAXIMUS
GLUTEUS MAXIMUS

The skin of your fingertips is ridged and sensitive.

Gluteus maximus
You sit on your gluteus maximus, the largest and most powerful muscle in your body.

Stand tall
The soleus at the back of your calf helps steady your legs when you are standing.

Hairy human
Hair covers every inch of your body, except for your lips, the palms of your hands, and the bottoms of your feet.

BICEPS FEMORIS
SEMITENDINOUS
SEMIMEMBRANOSUS
BICEPS FEMORIS
RECTUS FEMORIS
SARTORIUS
VASTUS MEDIALIS
RECTUS FEMORIS
SARTORIUS
RECTUS FEMORIS
VASTUS LATERALIS

Hamstrings
The group of muscles at the back of your thigh is called the hamstrings.

GASTROCNEMIUS
GASTROCNEMIUS
SOLEUS
SOLEUS
PERONEUS BREVIS
EXTENSOR MUSCLE
TIBIALIS ANTERIOR

TIBIALIS ANTERIOR
GASTROCNEMIUS
TIBIALIS ANTERIOR

Gastrocnemius
This muscle, which forms the calf, is used to raise your knee and lift your heel.

The skin on the bottoms of your feet is thick and tough.

Extensor muscle

Abductor muscle

Wrinkly skin
Skin over joints such as the knee is extra-flexible and wrinkles easily.

Control and Maintenance

YOU NEED A CONSTANT SUPPLY of energy to power your body. Your digestive and respiratory systems pass fuel and oxygen to your blood; the circulatory, lymphatic, and excretory systems deliver these substances to cells and take away wastes. Coordinating and controlling every action are the nervous and endocrine systems.

NERVOUS AND ENDOCRINE SYSTEMS

The nervous system connects your entire body with its master control center, the brain. Sensory nerves carry signals from your sense organs to your brain; once the brain decides what to do, it sends messages to your muscles along motor nerves. This system works closely with the endocrine system, which uses chemical messengers called hormones to control many body processes, as well as growth and development.

Sensory signals
Your brain gets information from outside of your body from the organs of your main senses – sight, hearing, smell, taste, touch, and balance.

Adrenal glands
When you are angry or frightened, these glands tell your body to get ready for action.

CIRCULATORY SYSTEM

Fresh, oxygen-carrying blood pumped from the heart reaches all parts of your body through tubes called arteries. These branch into tiny capillaries, where blood gives up oxygen and nutrients to the surroundings and takes in wastes for disposal. Tubes known as veins collect the used blood and send it back to the heart.

The doughnut-shaped red cells floating in your blood carry oxygen; the lumpy white cells fight infection.

Eye and optic nerve *for sight*

Thyroid
This gland helps regulate body growth.

Pituitary
Found just below the brain, this gland releases hormones to control other glands.

BRAIN

THORACIC NERVES

SPINAL CORD

PANCREAS

LUMBAR NERVES

SACRAL NERVES

Carotid artery
Blood reaches your brain through this artery.

Aorta
The aorta carries fresh blood from the heart to the rest of your body.

Jugular vein
Deep in the neck, this vein returns blood from the head to the heart.

HEART

Heart
This muscular, two-part pump keeps blood circulating around your body.

Vena cava
Used blood from your organs pours into the vena cava for the return journey to your heart.

Touch signals
Senses are more complex than they seem. The sense of touch in your fingertips involves pressure, heat, cold, and pain.

Femoral artery *to leg*

Extra push
The massaging movements of the calf muscles help pump blood in the lower legs upward, against the pull of gravity.

The great saphenous vein is the longest in the body.

Motor nerves *control the muscles of the lower body.*

Toe nerves
Sensory nerves stretch right into your toetips, telling you when you have stubbed your toe.

A SENSE OF TASTE

Your tongue is an extremely mobile muscle that enables you to taste food, move it around as you chew, push it back into your pharynx (throat) when swallowing, and speak up to ask for more! The tongue's rough surface is covered with tiny bumps called papillae. On and between these are microscopic onion-shaped bunches of cells, the taste buds. These detect food flavors and send signals to the taste center in your brain. Although you may enjoy many different flavors, your taste buds can detect only four basic tastes: sweet, salty, bitter, and sour.

The lingual and palatine tonsils contain germ-killing cells.

The epiglottis covers your windpipe when you swallow food.

EPIGLOTTIS

PALATINE TONSIL

LINGUAL TONSIL

PALATINE TONSIL

BITTER

SOUR

SALT

SWEET

SOUR

APEX OF TONGUE

Rear of tongue senses bitter tastes.

Side of tongue detects sour tastes.

Salty tastes are detected just to the sides of the apex (tip).

Tip of tongue senses sweet tastes.

LYMPHATIC SYSTEM

This is your body's "other" circulatory system. Its branching network of vessels contains lymph, a thin, milky fluid. Lymph carries some nutrients around the body, especially fats. It also distributes germ-fighting white cells. Lymph is formed from bits of blood and other body liquids that ooze and collect in the spaces between cells. The system channels the fluid into vessels throughout your body, and eventually empties it back into your bloodstream.

Lymph nodes
Sometimes called glands, these are enlargements of lymph vessels. Blood is cleaned and filtered in the nodes, and germ-fighting cells gather there during illness.

Cervical lymph nodes
When you have a sore throat, white blood cells mass together in these nodes to fight the infection. As a result, your throat can feel swollen and tender.

Thymus
Lymph carries white blood cells to this twin-lobed organ, where they multiply and change into special infection-fighting cells.

Inguinal nodes
The network of lymph vessels in your lower body passes lymph into the bean-sized inguinal nodes deep in your groin.

Popliteal nodes
These nodes, clustered behind the knee, help collect excess fluids from your foot and leg.

Go with the flow
Lymph has no pump of its own. Its flow depends on pressure from your blood system and the massaging effects of your muscles.

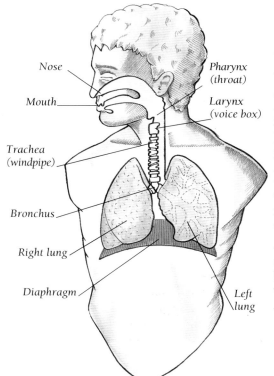

Nose
Mouth
Pharynx (throat)
Larynx (voice box)
Trachea (windpipe)
Bronchus
Right lung
Diaphragm
Left lung

Lymph vessels of lower leg and foot

RESPIRATORY SYSTEM

The main job of this system is to draw oxygen from the air into your body. When you breathe in, you suck fresh air through your trachea and down into your two lungs. The thin linings and huge surface area of the lungs enable them to absorb the maximum amount of oxygen, which passes to your blood. At the same time, waste carbon dioxide is given off from your blood into the air in your lungs. When you breathe out, these wastes are carried away.

DIGESTIVE SYSTEM

Nutrients in the food you eat contain the energy you need to live and the building blocks for the growth and repair of your body. The digestive system is designed to take in and process all kinds of foods, from soft vegetables to hard nuts and tough meats. Your teeth cut and chew the food; your stomach pulverizes it and bombards it with powerful digestive chemicals; your small intestine continues digestion and absorbs the dissolved nutrients; and your large intestine prepares the wastes for disposal.

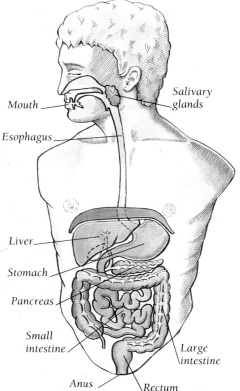

Mouth
Salivary glands
Esophagus
Liver
Stomach
Pancreas
Small intestine
Large intestine
Anus
Rectum

EXCRETORY SYSTEM

The digestive system rids your body of one kind of waste – digestive leftovers. The excretory system gets rid of different wastes – from your blood. Two kidneys filter waste chemicals and unwanted water from your blood, producing a fluid called urine. This trickles down tubes called ureters into a storage bag, the bladder. When you squeeze your bladder muscles, the urine is expelled by way of the urethra.

Renal vein
Right kidney
Inferior vena cava
Ureter
Bladder
Renal artery
Left kidney
Abdominal aorta
Urethra

The Head and Neck

SITTING ON THE TOP of your body, balanced on your neck, is the head. You will find most of the things that set you apart from others in this part of your body. Under its layers of skin, fat, and muscle lies the skull, a strong, bony structure that houses the brain – the nerve center of the body. Your senses of smell, hearing, taste, and sight are all located in your head, as are the parts of your body that you use to speak, think, and learn.

Peel back the skin, fat, and muscles of your head and neck, and this is what you would see: the front part of the head is a mass of about 30 muscles controlling the eyes, face, and mouth. Below the main part of the head are the muscles that bend and twist the neck and the major blood vessels that link the head with the heart.

GOING FOR THE JUGULAR

The large carotid artery carries blood to the main parts of the brain. The internal jugular vein brings most of this blood back to the heart. In humans and other animals, this vein runs down from below the ear toward the muscles of the neck. Because it is very near the surface of the skin, it is vulnerable. When a wild animal catches its prey, it may go for the throat and rip open the jugular vein or carotid artery. The brain's vital blood supply is cut off, and so much blood pours out that the victim soon dies.

Forehead muscle

The occipitofrontalis muscle is one of several sheets of muscle wrapping around the forehead. Its front part helps wrinkle the forehead and raise the eyebrows.

Nose muscle

The nasalis muscle in your nose has two parts. When you flare your nostrils, you use the alar part, which runs sideways. When you wrinkle your nose you use the transverse part, which runs diagonally.

Facial vein

The facial vein carries blood from your upper face. It goes down the side of your nose and under your eye. If it is damaged by a hard knock, it leaks blood. This causes a black eye.

VOCAL CORDS

The vocal cords, used for speaking and singing, are located in your throat. They are made of strips of tough, elastic tissue covered by a delicate membrane. Vocal cords are situated in the larynx, or voice box (right), which is made of cartilage and muscle tissue. You can feel your larynx if you press on the front of your throat. Muscles in the larynx move the cords – loosely for low sounds and stretched tightly for high sounds. The photographs below show the vocal cords as a doctor sees them, looking down the throat using an instrument called a laryngoscope.

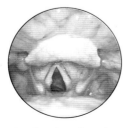

Cords pulled tightly together for speech

Cords relaxed and apart for breathing

FAT LAYER UNDER THE SKIN

OCCIPITOFRONTALIS

DURA

SKULL

PIA MATER COV

ORBICULARIS OCULI (EYELID MUSCLE)

EYE

NASALIS MUSCLE

FACIAL VEIN

FACIAL VEIN

CHEEKBONE

NASAL CAVITY

FACIAL ARTERY

SMALL CHEEK MUSCLE

LARGE CHEEK MUSCLE

HARD PALATE

UPPER LIP

LOWER JAW

TONGUE

HYOID BONE

EPIGLOTTIS

MEMBRANE

LOWER LIP

LOWER JAW

GENIOGLOSSUS MUSCLE (ROOT OF TONGUE)

MASSETER MUSCLE

THYROID CARTILAGE

CRICOID CARTILAGE

GENIOHYOID MUSCLE

HYOID BONE

vocal cords

TRACHEAL CARTILAGE

TRACHEAL MEMBRANE

NECK MUSCLE

NECK MUSCLE

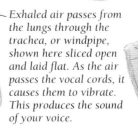

Exhaled air passes from the lungs through the trachea, or windpipe, shown here sliced open and laid flat. As the air passes the vocal cords, it causes them to vibrate. This produces the sound of your voice.

Shock-absorbing fluid

Between the pia and arachnoid meninges that cover and protect the brain is a thin layer of cerebrospinal fluid. This watery liquid circulates around the brain, helping to absorb shocks and jolts and preventing the brain from bumping into the bony skull.

M A T E R

A R A C H N O I D

ERING BRAIN

TEMPORALIS MUSCLE

S K U L L

S K I N

SUPERFICIAL TEMPORAL ARTERY

OCCIPITAL BELLY OF OCCIPITOFRONTALIS

OCCIPITAL BONE

EAR CANAL

SCALP VEIN

DEEP NECK MUSCLE

PAROTID GLAND

STERNOCLEIDOMASTOID MUSCLE

SPLENIUS CAPITIS MUSCLE

FATTY TISSUE

JUGULAR VEIN (External)

LEVATOR SCAPULAE MUSCLE

TRAPEZIUS MUSCLE

CAROTID ARTERY

JUGULAR VEIN (Internal)

OPEN WIDE OR SHUT UP!

Life would be very difficult without your lower jaw. Whether you are chatting or chewing, three sets of paired muscles are hard at work. The masseter and temporalis muscles under your jaw pull your mouth shut. The lateral pterygoid muscle pulls the rear of your lower jaw forward. This tilts the front of your lower jaw down, which opens your mouth.

Jaw open

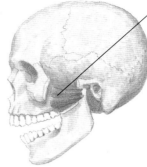

Lateral pterygoid tips jaw down

Jaw closed

Masseter clenches teeth

Temporalis pulls jaw up

Large skull bone

The whole skull is a complex jigsaw of 28 bones. One of the largest is the occipital bone, at the rear base of the calvaria, the "box" of bones surrounding the brain.

Outer ear canal

The outer ear canal is also called the ear tube. It is about an inch (25 mm) long. The ear tube collects sounds and funnels them to the eardrum.

Parotid gland

If you have had mumps, you know where your parotid gland is! This saliva-producing gland, just in front of your ear, swells painfully when infected by the mumps virus.

Nodding and shaking

To tilt your head from side to side or to turn your face around to the opposite side, you use the sternocleidomastoid muscle, located in your neck. When you look up or shrug your shoulders, you are using the trapezius muscle.

HOLD YOUR HEAD UP

A set of intertwined muscles supports and moves your head, neck, and shoulders. Your head weighs about 10 pounds (5 kg) and it takes a lot of effort to hold it up. Try lifting a bag of flour that heavy! A new baby's head is even larger and heavier in relation to its tiny body size. The muscles in its neck are not developed enough to support the head. That is why someone or something must constantly support a baby's head, until the muscles become strong enough to hold it up without help.

The Scalp and Skull

YOUR FACE TELLS other people about you – how you are feeling or what kind of mood you are in. But you also rely on special organs in this region – your eyes, ears, mouth, and nose – to tell you about the outside world. Under the surface of your face lies a network of muscles, blood vessels, nerves, and sense organs, all arranged around the solid structure of the skull.

The skull is made of 28 separate bones. These join solidly together during childhood at wiggly lines called sutures. Eight of these bones form a protective box, called the calvaria, around the brain. A further 14 bones give your face its shape, from the delicate lacrimal bone at the inner corner of your eye socket to the powerful mandible bone of the lower jaw. In addition, the smallest bones in your body are inside your skull: Deep in each ear are three tiny bones called ossicles, which help you hear.

The scalp is a specialized area of skin covering much of the sides and rear of your head. In most people, it contains about 100,000 tiny holes called hair follicles, from which hair grows.

THE BONES OF THE SKULL

This side view shows the separate bones of the skull, which fit together neatly like the pieces of a jigsaw puzzle. The skull bones cradle and protect the main sense organs as well as the brain. The temporal bone contains the delicate parts of the inner ear. Six bones on each side of the nose make a deep bowl, the eye socket. The olfactory organs, which you use to smell, are in the nasal cavity behind the two small nasal bones.

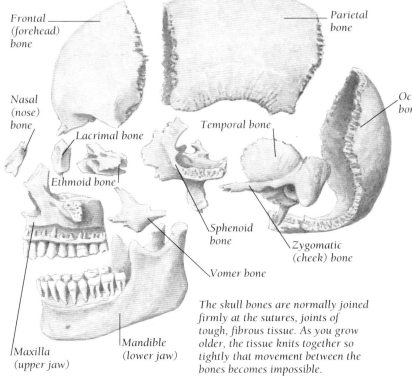

Frontal (forehead) bone

Nasal (nose) bone

Lacrimal bone

Ethmoid bone

Parietal bone

Occipital bone

Temporal bone

Sphenoid bone

Zygomatic (cheek) bone

Vomer bone

Maxilla (upper jaw)

Mandible (lower jaw)

The skull bones are normally joined firmly at the sutures, joints of tough, fibrous tissue. As you grow older, the tissue knits together so tightly that movement between the bones becomes impossible.

Facial veins
A system of veins carries blood down from the center top of the scalp to empty into the facial vein. The skin covering your face is richly supplied with blood vessels, which is why a cut on the head bleeds so much.

Thin skin
Your skin is not the same thickness all over your body. The thinnest is the skin covering your eyelids.

SUPRATROCHLEAR VEIN

SUPERFICIAL TEMPORAL ARTERY

FRONTAL SUPERIOR TEMPORAL VEIN

TEMPORALIS MUSCLE

ORBICULARIS OCULI (EYELID MUSCLE)

ZYGOMATICUS MINOR

SUPERFICIAL TEMPORAL VEIN

ZYGOMATICUS MAJOR

MASSETER

SKIN

FAT LAYER

FACIAL ARTERY

FACIAL VEIN

BUCCINATOR

MAXILLARY VEIN

SUBMENTAL ARTERY

SUBMENTAL VEIN

JUGULAR VEIN

MAXILLARY ARTERY

Blood vessels
A network of small arteries, mostly sandwiched between the skin and the underlying muscles, supplies blood to your face and scalp. When you feel hot or embarrassed, blood rushes into these arteries to help the extra body heat escape. As a result, your face gets red for a moment, a reaction called flushing or blushing.

Under the skin
Just below the skin, a layer of fat smooths the contours of your face and scalp. As it does throughout the body, the fatty layer helps slow heat loss so that your body temperature is less affected by cold weather.

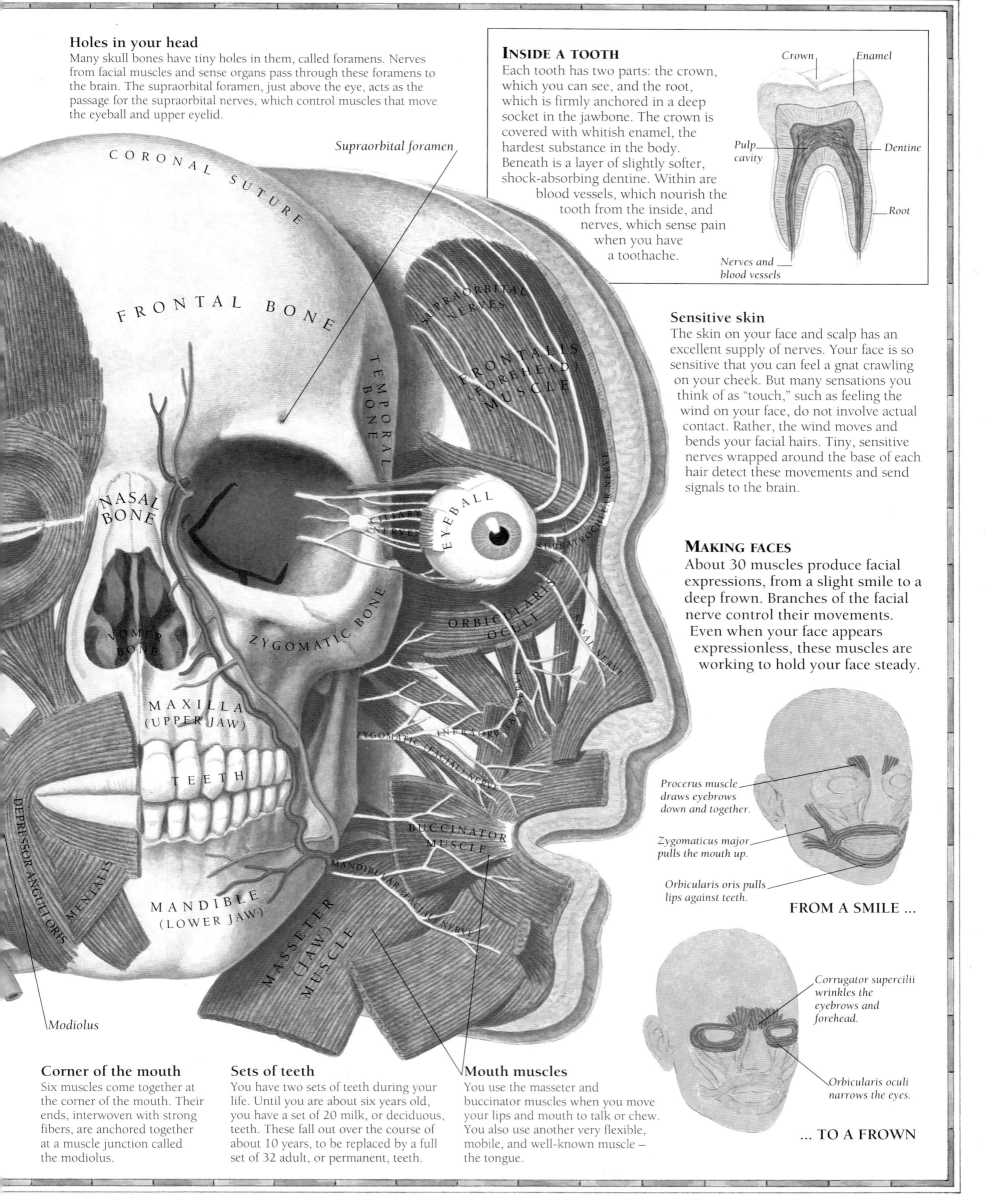

Holes in your head

Many skull bones have tiny holes in them, called foramens. Nerves from facial muscles and sense organs pass through these foramens to the brain. The supraorbital foramen, just above the eye, acts as the passage for the supraorbital nerves, which control muscles that move the eyeball and upper eyelid.

INSIDE A TOOTH

Each tooth has two parts: the crown, which you can see, and the root, which is firmly anchored in a deep socket in the jawbone. The crown is covered with whitish enamel, the hardest substance in the body. Beneath is a layer of slightly softer, shock-absorbing dentine. Within are blood vessels, which nourish the tooth from the inside, and nerves, which sense pain when you have a toothache.

Crown *Enamel*

Pulp cavity

Dentine

Root

Nerves and blood vessels

Sensitive skin

The skin on your face and scalp has an excellent supply of nerves. Your face is so sensitive that you can feel a gnat crawling on your cheek. But many sensations you think of as "touch," such as feeling the wind on your face, do not involve actual contact. Rather, the wind moves and bends your facial hairs. Tiny, sensitive nerves wrapped around the base of each hair detect these movements and send signals to the brain.

MAKING FACES

About 30 muscles produce facial expressions, from a slight smile to a deep frown. Branches of the facial nerve control their movements. Even when your face appears expressionless, these muscles are working to hold your face steady.

CORONAL SUTURE

Supraorbital foramen

FRONTAL BONE

TEMPORAL BONE

SUPRAORBITAL NERVES

FRONTALIS (FOREHEAD) MUSCLE

NASAL BONE

CILIARY NERVES

EYEBALL

SUPRATROCHLEAR NERVE

VOMER BONE

ZYGOMATIC BONE

ORBICULARIS OCULI

NASAL NERVE

MAXILLA (UPPER JAW)

ZYGOMATIC (FACIAL) NERVE

INFRAORBITAL

TEETH

BUCCINATOR MUSCLE

DEPRESSOR ANGULI ORIS

MENTALIS

MANDIBLE (LOWER JAW)

MANDIBULAR (FACIAL) NERVE

MASSETER (JAW) MUSCLE

Modiolus

Procerus muscle draws eyebrows down and together.

Zygomaticus major pulls the mouth up.

Orbicularis oris pulls lips against teeth.

FROM A SMILE ...

Corrugator supercilii wrinkles the eyebrows and forehead.

Orbicularis oculi narrows the eyes.

... TO A FROWN

Corner of the mouth

Six muscles come together at the corner of the mouth. Their ends, interwoven with strong fibers, are anchored together at a muscle junction called the modiolus.

Sets of teeth

You have two sets of teeth during your life. Until you are about six years old, you have a set of 20 milk, or deciduous, teeth. These fall out over the course of about 10 years, to be replaced by a full set of 32 adult, or permanent, teeth.

Mouth muscles

You use the masseter and buccinator muscles when you move your lips and mouth to talk or chew. You also use another very flexible, mobile, and well-known muscle – the tongue.

The Brain

YOUR BRAIN IS THE nerve center of your body. It weighs just 3 pounds (1.3 kg) – roughly as much as two large honeydew melons – yet it controls most of your body movements, and gathers and stores information so that you can think and learn. Your brain has the consistency of stiff gelatin and has more wrinkles than a giant walnut. It rests inside your upper skull within the calvaria, a "box" of bones. There it is safely supported and protected from bumps and jolts. For extra protection, three thin layers of membrane, the meninges, lie like a triple-decker sandwich between the outer surface of your brain and the inner surface of your skull bones.

The cerebrum makes up nine-tenths of your brain. Most of your brain's work is done within this wrinkled mass of nerve cells. The cerebrum is divided into two rounded halves, known as cerebral hemispheres. These two halves are joined by the corpus callosum, a "bridge" of nerve fibers. The remaining tenth of your brain, located under the cerebrum, includes the cerebellum, pons, and medulla. These merge into the top of the spinal cord.

Lobes

Several sulci (grooves) divide each cerebral hemisphere into five main areas, or lobes. These are the prefrontal, frontal, parietal (at the top), temporal (at the side), and occipital (at the back). Each lobe has its own group of mental functions; in addition, other functions are spread through several lobes.

Frontal sinus

The sinuses are air-filled cavities within the thick skull bones, joined by openings to the main airway inside the nose. When you have a cold, sinuses fill with mucus, causing that "stuffed up" feeling and, sometimes, pain.

OCCIPITOFRONTALIS (MUSCLE SHEET)

FRONTAL SINUS

NASAL CAVITY

NERVE CENTER

The brain sends and receives messages through nerves that run down into the spinal cord. There are also 12 pairs of nerves that join directly to the brain and branch out into the head and neck. These are known as cranial nerves. One pair, called the first cranial, or olfactory, nerve, is for smelling; the second cranial, or optic, nerve, extends from the eye and is used for seeing.

Optic nerve
Corpus callosum
Cerebrum
Cerebellum
Spinal cord

At the optic chiasma near the hypothalamus, the optic nerves split and cross.

OPTIC CHIASMA

Anterior part makes hormones.

Pituitary stalk connects pituitary to hypothalamus.

Blood vessels in the stalk carry hormones and other chemicals to and from the pituitary.

Posterior part of pituitary gland makes and stores hormones.

PITUITARY STALK
ANTERIOR LOBE
BLOOD VESSEL NETWORK
BLOOD VESSEL NETWORK
POSTERIOR LOBE

NERVE-HORMONE CONNECTION

The pituitary gland makes hormones for many other glands and organs. It also receives instructions from the hypothalamus, just above it. The hypothalamus, a network of nerves, monitors the levels of hormones and chemicals in the body. It also produces hormonelike chemicals, which it delivers to the pituitary gland.

GRAY MATTER

When you think about something, you are using the outer layers of your cerebral hemispheres, called the cerebral cortex. The cerebral cortex also analyzes signals from your senses. Its outermost layer is 0.1 in. (3 mm) of "gray matter," consisting of nerve cells and their short, interwoven branches. Beneath it is the white matter, mainly bundles of long fibers that link the parts of the brain to each other.

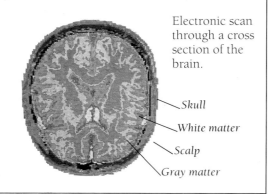

Electronic scan through a cross section of the brain.

Skull
White matter
Scalp
Gray matter

BRAIN MAP

On the outside, each cerebral hemisphere looks the same all over. In fact, it is divided into several different areas, or centers, each with its own job. Sensory centers receive nerve signals from your senses. Motor centers send signals out to your body muscles. The main body motor center is subdivided into parts that control your tongue, lips, face, fingers, and other body regions.

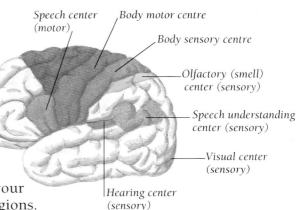

Speech center (motor)
Body motor centre
Body sensory centre
Olfactory (smell) center (sensory)
Speech understanding center (sensory)
Visual center (sensory)
Hearing center (sensory)

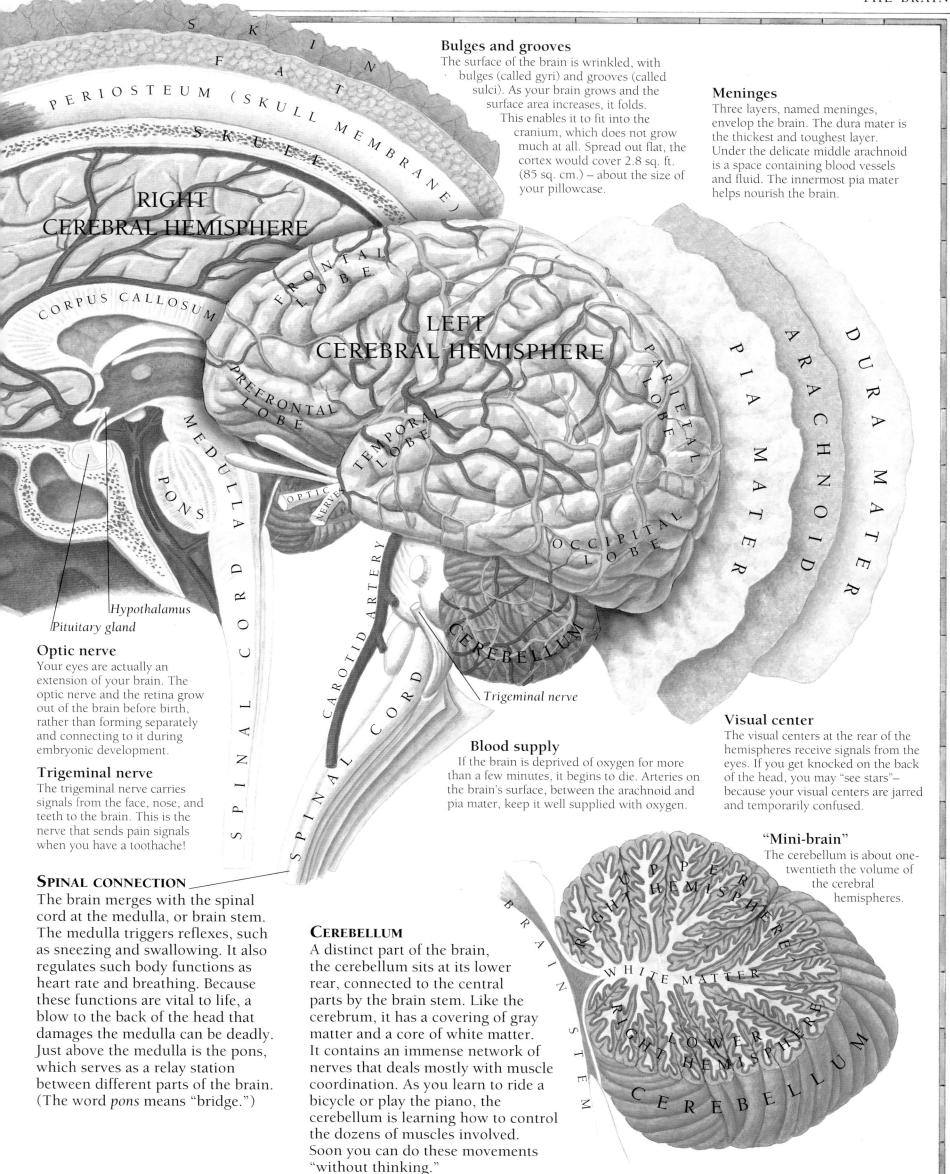

Bulges and grooves
The surface of the brain is wrinkled, with bulges (called gyri) and grooves (called sulci). As your brain grows and the surface area increases, it folds. This enables it to fit into the cranium, which does not grow much at all. Spread out flat, the cortex would cover 2.8 sq. ft. (85 sq. cm.) – about the size of your pillowcase.

Meninges
Three layers, named meninges, envelop the brain. The dura mater is the thickest and toughest layer. Under the delicate middle arachnoid is a space containing blood vessels and fluid. The innermost pia mater helps nourish the brain.

RIGHT CEREBRAL HEMISPHERE

CORPUS CALLOSUM

FRONTAL LOBE

LEFT CEREBRAL HEMISPHERE

PREFRONTAL LOBE

PARIETAL LOBE

PIA MATER

ARACHNOID

DURA MATER

MEDULLA

PONS

TEMPORAL LOBE

OPTIC NERVE

OCCIPITAL LOBE

Hypothalamus

Pituitary gland

SPINAL CORD

CAROTID ARTERY

SPINAL CORD

CEREBELLUM

Trigeminal nerve

Optic nerve
Your eyes are actually an extension of your brain. The optic nerve and the retina grow out of the brain before birth, rather than forming separately and connecting to it during embryonic development.

Trigeminal nerve
The trigeminal nerve carries signals from the face, nose, and teeth to the brain. This is the nerve that sends pain signals when you have a toothache!

SPINAL CONNECTION
The brain merges with the spinal cord at the medulla, or brain stem. The medulla triggers reflexes, such as sneezing and swallowing. It also regulates such body functions as heart rate and breathing. Because these functions are vital to life, a blow to the back of the head that damages the medulla can be deadly. Just above the medulla is the pons, which serves as a relay station between different parts of the brain. (The word *pons* means "bridge.")

CEREBELLUM
A distinct part of the brain, the cerebellum sits at its lower rear, connected to the central parts by the brain stem. Like the cerebrum, it has a covering of gray matter and a core of white matter. It contains an immense network of nerves that deals mostly with muscle coordination. As you learn to ride a bicycle or play the piano, the cerebellum is learning how to control the dozens of muscles involved. Soon you can do these movements "without thinking."

Blood supply
If the brain is deprived of oxygen for more than a few minutes, it begins to die. Arteries on the brain's surface, between the arachnoid and pia mater, keep it well supplied with oxygen.

Visual center
The visual centers at the rear of the hemispheres receive signals from the eyes. If you get knocked on the back of the head, you may "see stars"– because your visual centers are jarred and temporarily confused.

"Mini-brain"
The cerebellum is about one-twentieth the volume of the cerebral hemispheres.

BRAIN STEM

RIGHT UPPER HEMISPHERE

WHITE MATTER

RIGHT LOWER HEMISPHERE

CEREBELLUM

The Eye

YOU RELY ON YOUR EYES to guide you in almost everything you do. These delicate organs measure just 1 in. (25 mm) across and are filled with a transparent gelatinlike substance. Deep bowls in the skull bones, the eye sockets, or orbits, protect your eyeballs from damage. Exposed only at the front to allow you to see, the eyes are also protected by eyelids, thin folds that can close rapidly.

Every time you blink, tear fluid washes over the exposed surface. A moist, clear membrane called the conjunctiva also provides lubrication. The sclera, a tough, white skin, covers most of the rest of the eyeball. Inside the sclera is a blood-rich layer called the choroid, which nourishes the other layers inside the eye. Within the choroid is the retina. There, 130 million cells collect light and images, providing you with the pictures of the world you see.

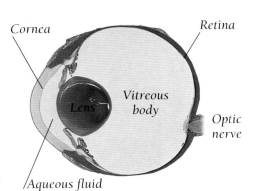

Cornea Retina Vitreous body Lens Optic nerve Aqueous fluid

EYES LEFT
This cross section shows the lens at the left, and the optic nerve at the right. The retina, which detects light, is microscopically thin. The vitreous body is a clear, yellowish gelatin which allows light to pass through to the retina.

THE PUPIL
The hole in the center of the iris is called the pupil. In dim light, the pupil enlarges to let in as much light as possible, so you can see. In bright light, it shrinks, protecting the nerve cells at the back of the eye. Using an instrument called an ophthalmoscope, a doctor can look through the pupil and see the retina, with blood vessels branching across it, as well as the optic disc, where the optic nerve leaves the eye. This is called the blind spot because it has no nerve cells for seeing.

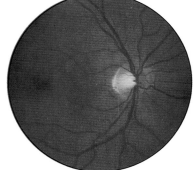

This is how the retina appears when viewed through an ophthalmoscope.

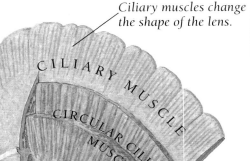

Ciliary muscles change the shape of the lens.

CILIARY MUSCLE

CIRCULAR CILIARY MUSCLE

Ciliary ligaments hold the lens in place.

The flexible, transparent lens is made of layers of protein.

LENS

IRIS

PUPIL

CENTER OF LENS

CILIARY PROCESS

CILIARY MUSCLE

Ciliary processes produce aqueous fluid and help support lens.

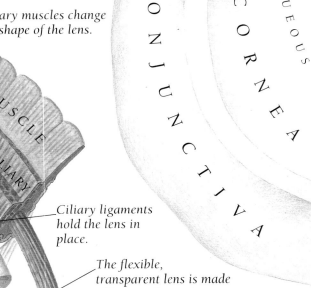

FRONTAL SINUS

FRONTAL BONE

FATTY

TEAR GLAND

SKIN

EYELID

UPPER TARSAL SHEET

EYELASH

SCLERA

CHOROID

LENS

IRIS

PUPIL

CONJUNCTIVA

CORNEA

AQUEOUS FLUID

LOWER TARSAL SHEET

EYELID

CILIARY MUSCLE

THE EXPOSED EYE
Under the conjunctiva, on the exposed part of the eye (above), is the clear, domed cornea. The cornea helps focus light. It is supported by the aqueous fluid. Under this is the iris, a circular network of muscles that change the size of the pupil. The iris also has pigments which determine the color of your eyes. Behind the iris are the lens and the ciliary muscles.

Inside the Ear

From quiet whispers to noisy crashes, or deep rumbles to high squeaks, your ears pick up a vast array of sounds. Your ears and brain together provide your sense of hearing. Ears convert sound waves into electrical nerve impulses, which speed to the brain for interpretation. They also help you keep your balance by telling your brain which way up you are.

What we usually call the ear, the flap of curved skin on the side of the head, does not hear. It catches sound waves and funnels them into an S-shaped tunnel, the outer ear canal. The canal leads deep inside the skull, where the sound waves reach the parts of the ear that do the hearing. The conversion of sounds into electrical impulses takes place in a tiny fluid-filled spiral structure, the cochlea, which could sit on your thumbnail like a small snail. Attached to the cochlea are three C-shaped canals, which help you keep your balance.

PEER THROUGH AN EAR

The three main areas of each ear, called the outer, middle, and inner ears, are exposed in the picture on the right. The outer ear is made up of the curved flap of skin on the outside of your head and the ear canal. The canal stretches to the middle ear, a tiny chamber containing the three auditory (hearing) bones. Beyond these bones are the structures of the inner ear, the cochlea and semicircular canals.

Ear trumpet

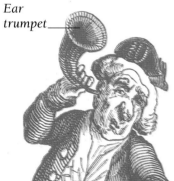

HEARING AID

Your ear flap is also called the auricle or pinna. Its curved rims, the outer and inner helices, help collect sounds. In the past, people who had trouble hearing sometimes used an ear trumpet. This device collects and funnels sound waves to the ear.

The ear canal

The hole in the middle of your ear is the entrance to the ear canal, also known as the external auditory canal. Sound waves travel through this 1 in. (2.5 cm) passageway before reaching the eardrum.

Wax in your ears

Ear wax, or cerumen, is made by glands in the skin that lines the ear canal. The sticky wax works with the hairs in the canal to trap dirt and dust before it can reach the delicate eardrum.

Safe and sound

The delicate internal parts of your ear are well protected by the thick skull bones surrounding them.

SKIN OF SCALP

FATTY LAYER

TEMPORAL BONE OF SKULL

H E L I X (OUTER RIM)

ANTIHELIX (INNER RIM)

CARTILAGE

CARTILAGE

EXTERNAL AUDITORY CANAL

EAR WAX

AIR TO SOLID TO LIQUID

Sound reaches your ear as waves of vibrating air molecules. When these vibrations strike and rattle the eardrum, its movements set the three linked ear bones in the middle ear vibrating. The third bone passes the vibrations to the fluid inside the cochlea, in the inner ear. This process is called air conduction.

Some sounds, like that of your own voice, reach the inner ear through your skull bones, a process known as bone conduction. When you listen to your voice on a tape recording, it may seem unfamiliar and strange. That's because the sound is reaching your ears through air instead of partly through your skull bones, as you are used to hearing it.

1. The ear flap catches and funnels sound waves into the ear.

2. The sound waves hit your flexible eardrum and make it rattle back and forth.

Cochlea shown straightened out

3. Three ossicles (ear bones) pick up these vibrations and transmit them to the oval window.

4. Vibrations of the oval window cause ripples in the liquid inside the cochlea.

Ceruminous (ear wax) gland

LOBULE (EARLOBE)

Earlobe

The thick skin of your earlobe, or lobule, wraps around fat and connective tissue.

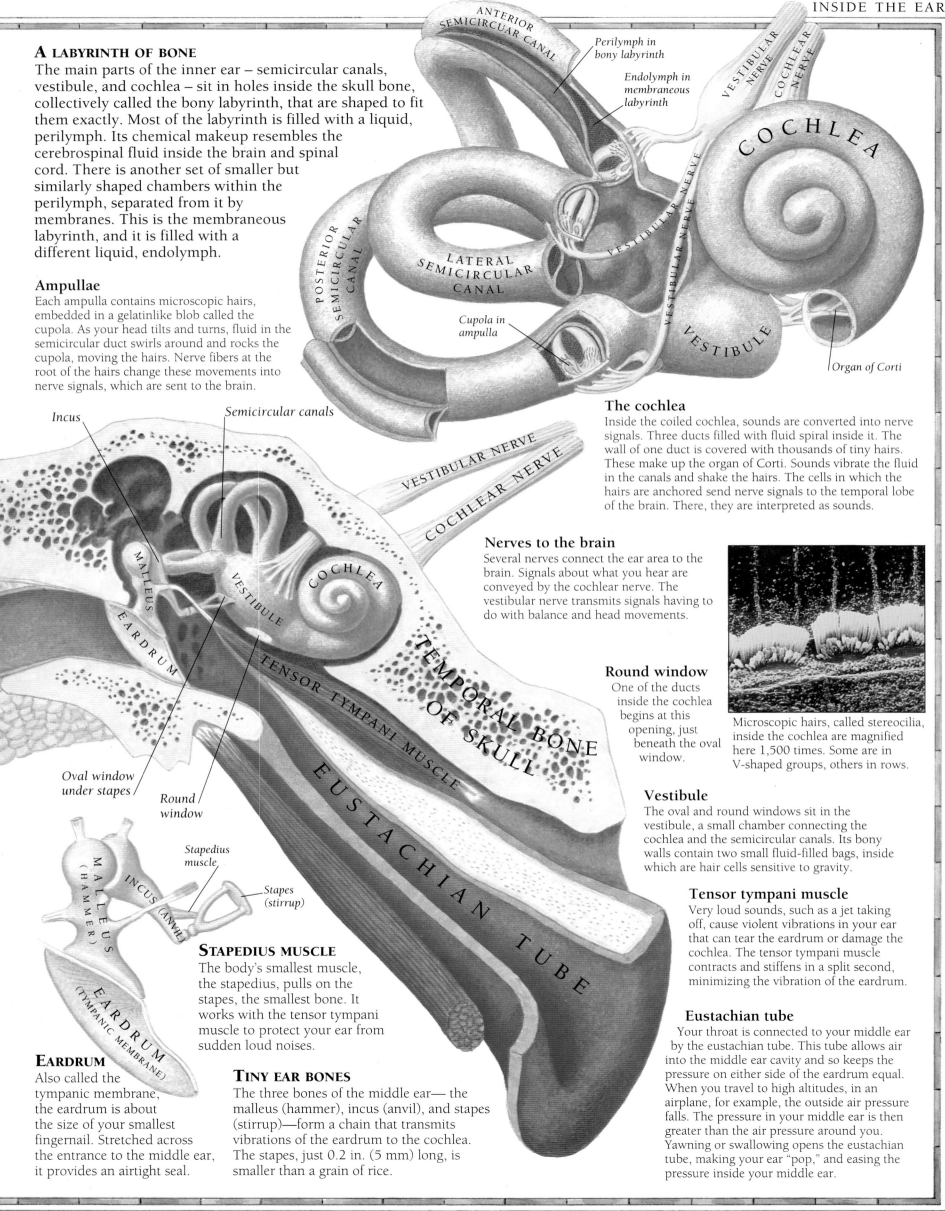

A LABYRINTH OF BONE

The main parts of the inner ear – semicircular canals, vestibule, and cochlea – sit in holes inside the skull bone, collectively called the bony labyrinth, that are shaped to fit them exactly. Most of the labyrinth is filled with a liquid, perilymph. Its chemical makeup resembles the cerebrospinal fluid inside the brain and spinal cord. There is another set of smaller but similarly shaped chambers within the perilymph, separated from it by membranes. This is the membraneous labyrinth, and it is filled with a different liquid, endolymph.

Ampullae

Each ampulla contains microscopic hairs, embedded in a gelatinlike blob called the cupola. As your head tilts and turns, fluid in the semicircular duct swirls around and rocks the cupola, moving the hairs. Nerve fibers at the root of the hairs change these movements into nerve signals, which are sent to the brain.

Incus

Semicircular canals

ANTERIOR SEMICIRCULAR CANAL

Perilymph in bony labyrinth

Endolymph in membraneous labyrinth

VESTIBULAR NERVE

COCHLEAR NERVE

COCHLEA

POSTERIOR SEMICIRCULAR CANAL

LATERAL SEMICIRCULAR CANAL

VESTIBULAR NERVE

Cupola in ampulla

VESTIBULE

Organ of Corti

The cochlea

Inside the coiled cochlea, sounds are converted into nerve signals. Three ducts filled with fluid spiral inside it. The wall of one duct is covered with thousands of tiny hairs. These make up the organ of Corti. Sounds vibrate the fluid in the canals and shake the hairs. The cells in which the hairs are anchored send nerve signals to the temporal lobe of the brain. There, they are interpreted as sounds.

VESTIBULAR NERVE

COCHLEAR NERVE

MALLEUS

EARDRUM

VESTIBULE

COCHLEA

TEMPORAL BONE OF SKULL

TENSOR TYMPANI MUSCLE

EUSTACHIAN TUBE

Nerves to the brain

Several nerves connect the ear area to the brain. Signals about what you hear are conveyed by the cochlear nerve. The vestibular nerve transmits signals having to do with balance and head movements.

Round window

One of the ducts inside the cochlea begins at this opening, just beneath the oval window.

Oval window under stapes

Round window

Microscopic hairs, called stereocilia, inside the cochlea are magnified here 1,500 times. Some are in V-shaped groups, others in rows.

Vestibule

The oval and round windows sit in the vestibule, a small chamber connecting the cochlea and the semicircular canals. Its bony walls contain two small fluid-filled bags, inside which are hair cells sensitive to gravity.

Tensor tympani muscle

Very loud sounds, such as a jet taking off, cause violent vibrations in your ear that can tear the eardrum or damage the cochlea. The tensor tympani muscle contracts and stiffens in a split second, minimizing the vibration of the eardrum.

MALLEUS (HAMMER)

INCUS (ANVIL)

Stapedius muscle

Stapes (stirrup)

EARDRUM (TYMPANIC MEMBRANE)

STAPEDIUS MUSCLE

The body's smallest muscle, the stapedius, pulls on the stapes, the smallest bone. It works with the tensor tympani muscle to protect your ear from sudden loud noises.

EARDRUM

Also called the tympanic membrane, the eardrum is about the size of your smallest fingernail. Stretched across the entrance to the middle ear, it provides an airtight seal.

TINY EAR BONES

The three bones of the middle ear— the malleus (hammer), incus (anvil), and stapes (stirrup)—form a chain that transmits vibrations of the eardrum to the cochlea. The stapes, just 0.2 in. (5 mm) long, is smaller than a grain of rice.

Eustachian tube

Your throat is connected to your middle ear by the eustachian tube. This tube allows air into the middle ear cavity and so keeps the pressure on either side of the eardrum equal. When you travel to high altitudes, in an airplane, for example, the outside air pressure falls. The pressure in your middle ear is then greater than the air pressure around you. Yawning or swallowing opens the eustachian tube, making your ear "pop," and easing the pressure inside your middle ear.

The Neck

IMAGINE HAVING A permanent stiff neck! You would not be able to turn your head to look around or to pinpoint sounds, unless you moved your whole body. You would not even be able to nod to say "yes." The neck provides a strong and flexible stalk for the head, allowing it to tilt and twist. To hold your head steady and move your neck, you rely on sets of muscles that link the neck with the spine, ribs, and shoulder bones.

Three vital sets of pipework pass through the neck. One is the tunnel down the middle of the spine, which houses the spinal cord, the main nerve in the body. The second pipe is the trachea, or windpipe, which conveys air to and from the lungs. The third pipe is the esophagus. When you swallow, chewed food from the mouth passes down the esophagus, through the chest, to the stomach. All three sets of pipework are stretchy and pliable, bending easily as you move. There are also numerous blood vessels, nerves, and lymph vessels in the neck. This concentration of essential airways, nerves, and vessels has meant that the neck is a prime target for enemies and executioners, from the scaffold to the guillotine.

FORAMEN MAGNUM

Looking at the skull from below, you can see a large hole. This is called the foramen magnum. The spinal cord passes through this hole to join the base of the brain.

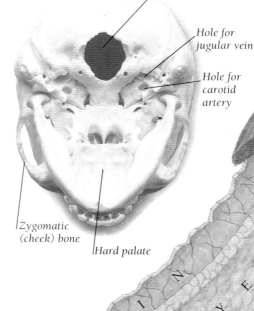

Foramen magnum

Hole for jugular vein

Hole for carotid artery

Zygomatic (cheek) bone

Hard palate

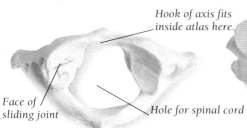

Hook of axis fits inside atlas here.

Face of sliding joint

Hole for spinal cord

Peglike hook (dens)

ATLAS

This bone sits at the top of the spinal column. It is more ring-shaped than the others. Sliding joints on each side of it allow the head to nod up and down.

AXIS

Directly under the atlas is the axis. It has a peglike hook (the dens) that fits into a notch in the atlas. This peg-and-ring system allows the head to swivel from side to side.

NECK MUSCLES

Each pair of neck muscles pulls the skull in a different way. When you look up, the vertical muscles at the back of your neck contract. When you look down, the muscles at the front contract. Other neck muscles run diagonally around the neck. They pull the skull around, enabling you to twist your head. At the same time, opposing muscles tense so that the face is kept steady and looking horizontally, rather than being tilted down. So just shaking your head to say no requires the coordination of dozens of muscles.

The two splenius capitis muscles, shown here, are one of the sets of muscles that join the base of the skull and the spine. They are used to rotate and tilt the head from side to side.

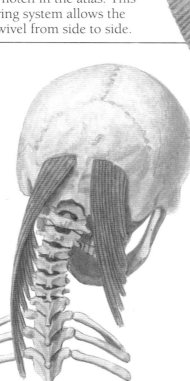

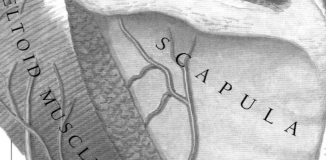

Levator scapulae

This long muscle is fixed to the atlas, axis, and neck backbones (vertebrae) above, and to the shoulder blade (scapula) below. The levator scapulae (which means "shoulder blade lifter") tenses up, becoming hard and stiff, when you carry a weight on your shoulder.

Spinal bones

Most of the spinal vertebrae have two flanges, or wings, one on either side, called transverse processes. These are anchor points for the spinal muscles.

Spinal nerves

Thirty-one pairs of spinal nerves emerge from the spinal cord inside the spine. The nerves that supply the upper part of the body emerge from a bulge at the top of the spinal cord called the cervical enlargement.

SEMISPINALIS CAPITIS MUSCLE

SPLENIUS CAPITIS MUSCLE

LEVATOR SCAPULAE MUSCLE

SKIN

FAT LAYER

BACK MUSCLE

DELTOID MUSCLE

SCAPULA

BACK MUSCLE

SPINAL NERVE ROOTS

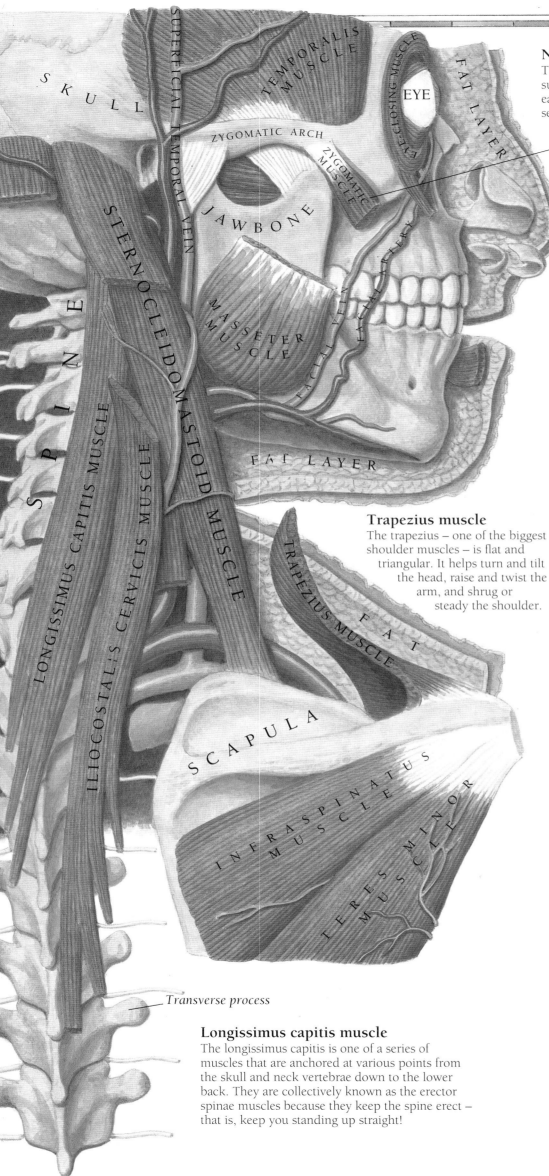

SKULL

SUPERFICIAL TEMPORAL VEIN

TEMPORALIS MUSCLE

EYE-CLOSING MUSCLE

EYE

FAT LAYER

ZYGOMATIC ARCH

ZYGOMATIC MUSCLE

JAWBONE

SPINE

STERNOCLEIDOMASTOID MUSCLE

LONGISSIMUS CAPITIS MUSCLE

ILIOCOSTALIS CERVICIS MUSCLE

MASSETER MUSCLE

FACIAL VEIN

FACIAL ARTERY

FAT LAYER

TRAPEZIUS MUSCLE

FAT

SCAPULA

INFRASPINATUS MUSCLE

TERES MINOR MUSCLE

Transverse process

Trapezius muscle

The trapezius – one of the biggest shoulder muscles – is flat and triangular. It helps turn and tilt the head, raise and twist the arm, and shrug or steady the shoulder.

Longissimus capitis muscle

The longissimus capitis is one of a series of muscles that are anchored at various points from the skull and neck vertebrae down to the lower back. They are collectively known as the erector spinae muscles because they keep the spine erect – that is, keep you standing up straight!

No nose bones

The front part of the nose does not contain bones. It is supported by a framework of nine cartilages, joined to each other and to the skull bones. One of these, the septal cartilage, divides the nostrils.

Cheek muscle

Zygomatic is just another word for "cheek." So, to smile, you use your zygomaticus major muscle, which connects the corner of your mouth to your zygomatic bone. With other muscles, it pulls the lips wider and upward, into a grin.

ESOPHAGUS AND TRACHEA

Air can enter the body through both the nose and the mouth. Food comes through the mouth. The passageways from the nose and mouth join together behind the tongue to form the throat, or pharynx. Farther down they split again, into the esophagus, for food, and the trachea, for air, with the larynx at its top.

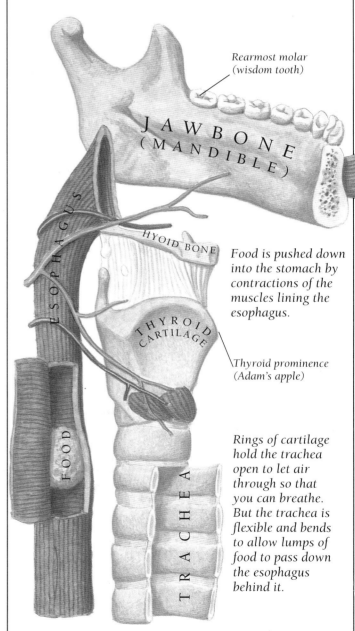

Rearmost molar (wisdom tooth)

JAWBONE (MANDIBLE)

ESOPHAGUS

HYOID BONE

THYROID CARTILAGE

FOOD

TRACHEA

Food is pushed down into the stomach by contractions of the muscles lining the esophagus.

Thyroid prominence (Adam's apple)

Rings of cartilage hold the trachea open to let air through so that you can breathe. But the trachea is flexible and bends to allow lumps of food to pass down the esophagus behind it.

SWALLOWING

The esophagus is normally squashed flat by internal body pressure. When you swallow, muscles arranged in circles within the wall of the esophagus contract in sequence. The traveling waves of contraction push food or drink downward, at the speed of about 1-2 in. (3-5 cm) each second.

When food enters the pharynx, the epiglottis swings across the entrance of the trachea to prevent the food from entering it. If something you eat "goes down the wrong tube," coughing forces air up the trachea, which loosens the food.

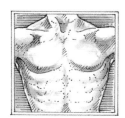

The Upper Torso

UNDERNEATH THE SKIN of your chest lies your body's powerhouse: the tireless team of the heart and lungs, working together to supply your entire body with fresh, oxygen-rich blood. A network of broad, flat muscles covers the movable bony cage formed by the ribs. The rib cage encloses and protects the soft, spongy lungs and pumping heart. Two vertical bony structures, the sternum (breastbone) at the front and the spinal column at the rear, act as girders to provide strength for the rib cage. Joints between the ribs, sternum, and spinal column allow the cage to change shape, so that the lungs can expand and contract as you breathe.

The cone-shaped area of your chest is also known as the thorax, and the belly below it is termed the abdomen. The two sections are divided just below your lungs by the diaphragm, a powerful sheet of muscle shaped like an upside-down bowl.

Inside the chest
Your chest must be strong enough to protect the delicate organs within, yet flexible enough to move as you breathe. The sheetlike layers of muscle anchored to your collarbone, or clavicle, contract to lift and expand your chest as you breathe in and relax as you breathe out.

MAMMARY GLAND
Everyone has mammary glands, but they are not highly developed in children and men. A woman's glands become active after childbirth, making milk to feed the baby. Each mammary gland (as shown on the right) has about 20 rounded lobes, held together by loose connective tissue. Each lobe contains numerous milk-making lobules. Narrow tubes, called lactiferous ducts, carry the milk into tiny openings in the nipple.

Alveoli
The milk made in the grapelike clusters of the alveoli glands is rich in nutrients and also protects the baby against some diseases.

Lactiferous duct
When a baby sucks the nipple, milk enters the lactiferous ducts and travels to tiny openings on its surface.

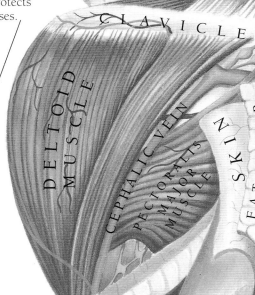

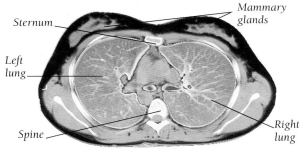

This computerized scan through a section of the chest shows the lungs, with the spine behind and the sternum and mammary glands in front.

A FLEXIBLE CAGE
Your rib cage is made of 12 pairs of springy C-shaped bones. The first pair is the shortest; the pairs below lengthen, then shorten again, to form the cage. Joined to vertebrae of the spine at the back, each rib arches around and down toward the sternum at the front. But the rib bones themselves do not reach the sternum. Instead, ribs are connected to the sternum by costal cartilage, tough, rubbery bars that give the rib cage extra flexibility.

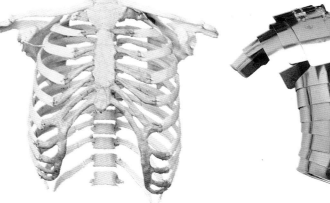

The dark yellow parts of this rib cage are costal cartilage.

This suit of armor copies the barred design of the rib cage.

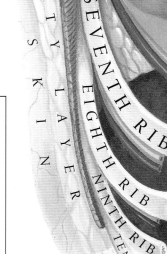

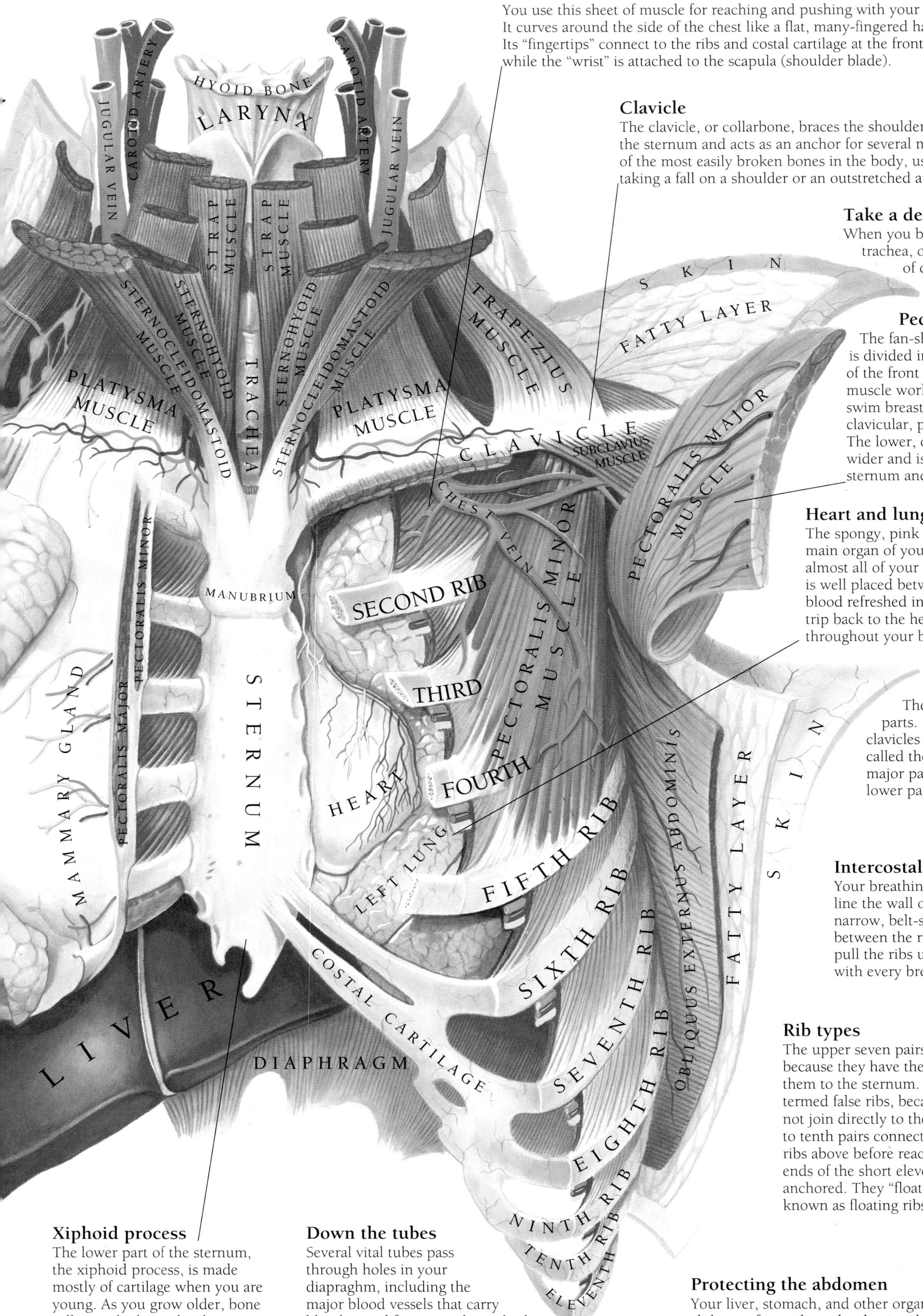

Serratus anterior
You use this sheet of muscle for reaching and pushing with your arms. It curves around the side of the chest like a flat, many-fingered hand. Its "fingertips" connect to the ribs and costal cartilage at the front, while the "wrist" is attached to the scapula (shoulder blade).

Clavicle
The clavicle, or collarbone, braces the shoulder joint against the sternum and acts as an anchor for several muscles. It is one of the most easily broken bones in the body, usually from taking a fall on a shoulder or an outstretched arm.

Take a deep breath
When you breathe in, air rushes through the trachea, or windpipe, a stretchy tube of cartilage and muscle, down to your lungs.

Pectoralis major muscle
The fan-shaped pectoralis major muscle is divided into two parts that cover most of the front of the chest. You can feel this muscle working when you row a boat or swim breaststroke. The upper, or clavicular, part is attached to the clavicle. The lower, or sternocostal, part is much wider and is anchored mainly to the sternum and costal cartilage.

Heart and lungs
The spongy, pink lobes of the lungs, the main organ of your respiratory system, fill almost all of your chest cavity. Your heart is well placed between them, so that blood refreshed in the lungs has a short trip back to the heart for circulation throughout your body.

Sternum
The breastbone has three main parts. Its upper plate, joined to the clavicles and the first pair of ribs, is called the manubrium. Below this is the major part, or sternal body. The small lower part is called the xiphoid process.

Intercostal muscles
Your breathing muscles, the intercostals, line the wall of the chest. These long, narrow, belt-shaped muscles are situated between the ribs. As they contract, they pull the ribs up to expand your chest with every breath.

Rib types
The upper seven pairs of ribs are called true ribs, because they have their own costal cartilage linking them to the sternum. The remaining pairs are termed false ribs, because their costal cartilage does not join directly to the sternum. Instead, the eighth to tenth pairs connect to the costal cartilage of the ribs above before reaching the sternum. The front ends of the short eleventh and twelfth pairs are not anchored. They "float" in the chest wall, so they are known as floating ribs.

Xiphoid process
The lower part of the sternum, the xiphoid process, is made mostly of cartilage when you are young. As you grow older, bone cells invade the xiphoid process, which hardens and turns to bone. This is called ossification.

Down the tubes
Several vital tubes pass through holes in your diapraghm, including the major blood vessels that carry blood to and from your lower body and the esophagus, which delivers food to your stomach.

Protecting the abdomen
Your liver, stomach, and other organs of the upper abdomen fit neatly under the upside-down bowl shape of the diaphragm. This brings them within the protective shield of the lower ribs.

Labels on illustration:
HYOID BONE
LARYNX
JUGULAR VEIN
CAROTID ARTERY
STRAP MUSCLE
CAROTID ARTERY
JUGULAR VEIN
STRAP MUSCLE
STERNOHYOID MUSCLE
STERNOCLEIDOMASTOID MUSCLE
TRACHEA
PLATYSMA MUSCLE
STERNOHYOID MUSCLE
STERNOCLEIDOMASTOID MUSCLE
PLATYSMA MUSCLE
TRAPEZIUS MUSCLE
SKIN
FATTY LAYER
CLAVICLE
SUBCLAVIUS MUSCLE
PECTORALIS MAJOR MUSCLE
CHEST VEIN
PECTORALIS MINOR
MANUBRIUM
SECOND RIB
PECTORALIS MINOR MUSCLE
THIRD
MAMMARY GLAND
PECTORALIS MAJOR
STERNUM
HEART
FOURTH
LEFT LUNG
FIFTH RIB
SIXTH RIB
SEVENTH RIB
EIGHTH RIB
OBLIQUUS EXTERNUS ABDOMINIS
FATTY LAYER
SKIN
LIVER
COSTAL CARTILAGE
DIAPHRAGM
NINTH RIB
TENTH RIB
ELEVENTH RIB

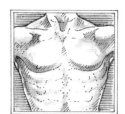

The Upper Torso – Back

MANY OF THE MUSCLES that give strength to the back of your upper torso are near the surface of the skin. In fact, you can trace their shapes on the well-developed upper back of the body-builder on the right. But if you could look beneath these muscles, you would uncover the real secret of your upper body's support: the strong, T-shaped structure formed by the spinal column, the rib cage, and the pair of scapulae (shoulder blades) linked to the clavicles (collarbones).

The ribs wrap up and around the front of your chest and meet the spinal column at the rear. The ends of each pair of ribs form joints with the vertebrae, or spinal bones. Together with the scapulae, these bones form a support system strong enough to bear the heavy weight of the muscles, bones, and organs of the head and chest, yet flexible enough to let you stretch up, reach across your body, bend double, and twist your body from side to side. A deep layer of muscles, some interwoven with the ribs and others linked to bony knobs on the spine, provides added flexibility and stability.

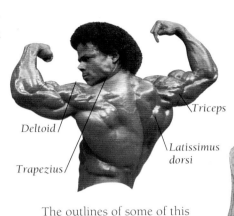

The outlines of some of this body-builder's superficial muscles – those just under the skin – are clearly visible. The muscles beneath these are called deep muscles.

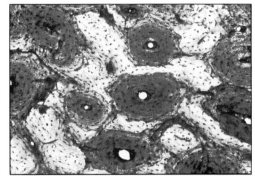

This is a micrograph of compact bone, like that forming the outer layer of a vertebra. Inside each round column of bone cells is a hollow space, called the haversian canal, containing nerves and blood and lymph vessels.

REAR OF THE RIB CAGE
A back view of the thorax (chest) clearly shows the pairs of ribs ranged down the spinal vertebrae, one pair for each thoracic vertebra. Each scapula joins to the clavicle and to the upper arm bone in the shoulder, but there are no direct joints between the scapula and ribs. This means the scapula is relatively free to slide around the back of the rib cage, contributing to the shoulder's great flexibility.

INSIDE A VERTEBRA
The typical vertebra has an outer shell of hard, dense bone, called compact bone. Within is the honeycomb of cancellous bone, which contains red bone marrow. All of your red blood cells and many of your white cells are made inside this soft, fatty tissue. A hormone signal starts the production of new cells in the marrow. There, they mature before they are released into circulation.

THE BACKBONE OF YOUR BODY
The movable joints between the rear end of a rib and the side of a vertebra are called costovertebral joints. In fact, each of these is a double joint. The end of the rib fits snugly into a shallow socket on the body (main part) of the vertebra, while a rear-facing part of the rib, called the costal neck and tubercle (bump), fits into the transverse process, or "side wing," of the vertebra.

INSIDE A RIB
Under its thin shell of compact bone, the rib is richly supplied with red bone marrow. Not all bones contain red marrow – it is found only within the ribs, vertebrae, sternum (breastbone), clavicles, scapulae, pelvis (hipbones), and skull bones.

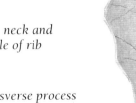

CANCELLOUS BONE

DISK

BODY of VERTEBRA

DISK

BODY of VERTEBRA

RIB

RIB

RIB

Costal neck and tubercle of rib

Transverse process

TRAPEZIUS

DELTOID

TERES MAJOR

SERRATUS ANTERIOR

SKIN

LATISSIMUS DORSI

FATTY LAYER

Deltoid

Triceps

Latissimus dorsi

Trapezius

Latissimus dorsi
The base of this long triangle of muscle is attached to the chest vertebrae, the lower ribs, and even to the hipbones far below. The muscle fibers at its tip meet under the scapula and join to the upper arm bone, the humerus, in the shoulder. You use the latissimus dorsi as you swing your arms back when jogging or reach up to grab something above your head.

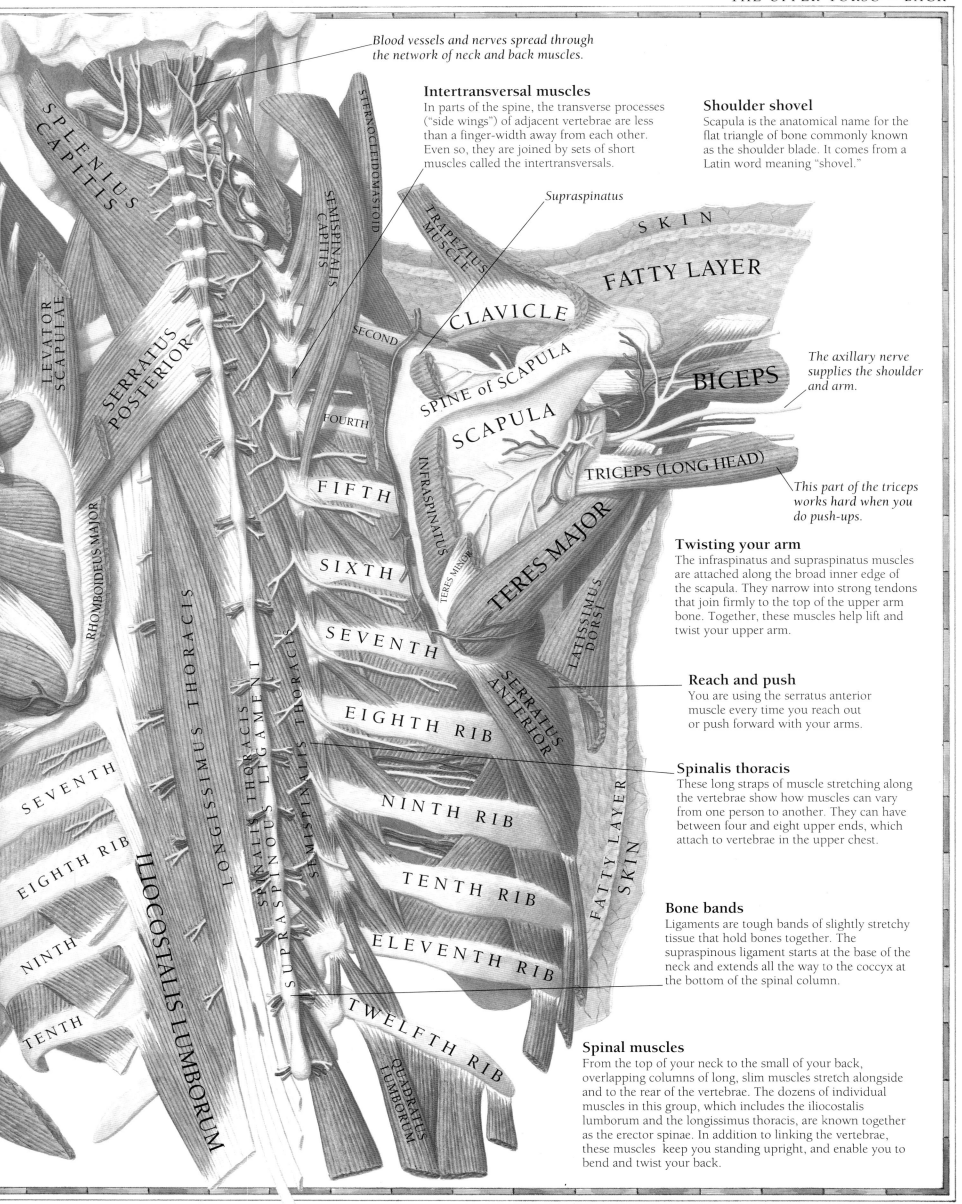

Blood vessels and nerves spread through the network of neck and back muscles.

SPLENIUS CAPITIS

LEVATOR SCAPULAE

SERRATUS POSTERIOR

RHOMBOIDEUS MAJOR

SEMISPINALIS CAPITIS

STERNOCLEIDOMASTOID

SECOND

FOURTH

FIFTH

SIXTH

SEVENTH

EIGHTH RIB

NINTH RIB

TENTH RIB

ELEVENTH RIB

TWELFTH RIB

LONGISSIMUS THORACIS

SPINALIS THORACIS

SPINOUS LIGAMENT

SEMISPINALIS THORACIS

SUPRASPINOUS

ILIOCOSTALIS LUMBORUM

SEVENTH

EIGHTH RIB

NINTH

TENTH

QUADRATUS LUMBORUM

TRAPEZIUS MUSCLE

CLAVICLE

SPINE of SCAPULA

SCAPULA

INFRASPINATUS

TERES MINOR

TERES MAJOR

SERRATUS ANTERIOR

LATISSIMUS DORSI

SKIN

FATTY LAYER

BICEPS

TRICEPS (LONG HEAD)

FATTY LAYER

SKIN

Intertransversal muscles
In parts of the spine, the transverse processes ("side wings") of adjacent vertebrae are less than a finger-width away from each other. Even so, they are joined by sets of short muscles called the intertransversals.

Supraspinatus

Shoulder shovel
Scapula is the anatomical name for the flat triangle of bone commonly known as the shoulder blade. It comes from a Latin word meaning "shovel."

The axillary nerve supplies the shoulder and arm.

This part of the triceps works hard when you do push-ups.

Twisting your arm
The infraspinatus and supraspinatus muscles are attached along the broad inner edge of the scapula. They narrow into strong tendons that join firmly to the top of the upper arm bone. Together, these muscles help lift and twist your upper arm.

Reach and push
You are using the serratus anterior muscle every time you reach out or push forward with your arms.

Spinalis thoracis
These long straps of muscle stretching along the vertebrae show how muscles can vary from one person to another. They can have between four and eight upper ends, which attach to vertebrae in the upper chest.

Bone bands
Ligaments are tough bands of slightly stretchy tissue that hold bones together. The supraspinous ligament starts at the base of the neck and extends all the way to the coccyx at the bottom of the spinal column.

Spinal muscles
From the top of your neck to the small of your back, overlapping columns of long, slim muscles stretch alongside and to the rear of the vertebrae. The dozens of individual muscles in this group, which includes the iliocostalis lumborum and the longissimus thoracis, are known together as the erector spinae. In addition to linking the vertebrae, these muscles keep you standing upright, and enable you to bend and twist your back.

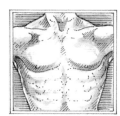

The Lungs

BREATHE IN AS DEEPLY AS YOU CAN. Watch your chest rise as your lungs fill with air. The lungs' vital function is to absorb oxygen from this air and pass it in dissolved form to the blood pulsing through them. The oxygen is exchanged for waste carbon dioxide, also dissolved in the blood, which is carried away in the air you breathe out. There is little time to spare in this process. If oxygen is lacking in the body, or if carbon dioxide builds up, death can follow within minutes.

The main bulk of the lungs is composed of tiny branching air tubes called bronchioles, which end in microscopic "air sacs" called alveoli. There are 300-350 million alveoli in each lung. Gas exchange – oxygen for carbon dioxide – takes place inside them, where air and blood are separated by a film of moisture and membrane only 0.00004 in. (0.0001 mm) thick.

THE LOBES OF YOUR LUNGS

There are two lungs inside your chest, but they are not exactly the same. The right one has three lobes, or sections. The left one has only two lobes and a hollowed-out area to make room for the heart. The upper tips (or apices) of the lungs reach above the inner ends of the clavicles (collarbones), almost into the neck. The lung bases rest on the dome-shaped sheet of the main breathing muscle, the diaphragm.

Pleural membranes

The lungs are enveloped within a smooth, double-layered membrane, the pleurae. The inner, or visceral, layer follows every contour of the lungs, wrapping around the lobes and the main airways. It folds back and over on itself to form the outer, or parietal, layer.

Between the two pleural layers is a tiny space containing slippery pleural fluid. The fluid works with the pleurae to lubricate the lungs as you breathe.

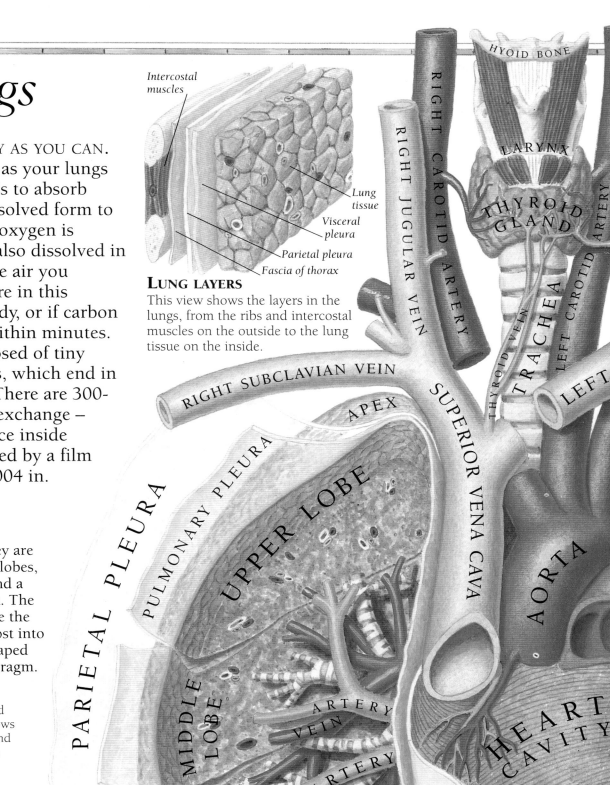

LUNG LAYERS
This view shows the layers in the lungs, from the ribs and intercostal muscles on the outside to the lung tissue on the inside.

Intercostal muscles
Lung tissue
Visceral pleura
Parietal pleura
Fascia of thorax

HYOID BONE
LARYNX
THYROID GLAND
RIGHT CAROTID ARTERY
LEFT CAROTID ARTERY
RIGHT JUGULAR VEIN
THYROID VEIN
TRACHEA
LEFT
RIGHT SUBCLAVIAN VEIN
APEX
SUPERIOR VENA CAVA
PARIETAL PLEURA
PULMONARY PLEURA
UPPER LOBE
AORTA
ARTERY
VEIN
MIDDLE LOBE
ARTERY
HEART CAVITY
LOWER LOBE
PERICARD
DIAPHRAGM
ABDOMINAL AORTA

BREATHING IN AND OUT

When you breathe in (inhale), your diaphragm tenses and its dome shape flattens, while your chest muscles pull the ribs up and out. Your chest cavity and lungs expand, as air rushes down the trachea and into the spongy lungs. When you breathe out (exhale), these two sets of muscles relax. Your ribs fall back, while the pressure from the abdominal contents below pushes your diaphragm back up. Air is forced out, and the lungs spring back to their starting size. When you are relaxed, you breathe about 15 times each minute.

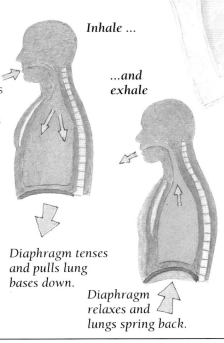

Inhale ...

...and exhale

Diaphragm tenses and pulls lung bases down.

Diaphragm relaxes and lungs spring back.

Pericardium
This tough membrane encloses the heart and holds it in place.

Air conditioning

Before breathed-in air travels to the lungs, it is "treated" inside your nose. Nasal hairs and sticky mucus trap dust and other particles. At the same time, cold air is warmed and dry air is moistened to match the conditions within the lung.

Trachea

Beneath the larynx is the trachea, the tube that carries air into the lungs. About 20 C-shaped hoops of cartilage help keep it open even when you swallow food or twist your neck.

Hairy lining

Thousands of tiny hairs called cilia line the walls of your airways. They move in waves to push mucus and specks of dust up out of the lungs and toward the throat.

Venule

Arteriole

Cartilage

Lung capacity

While you are reading this book, you are breathing in about a pint (one-half liter) of air, around 15 times a minute. But when you run for a bus, for example, your breathing rate can almost double and you breathe more deeply, so that you take in nearly five times as much air.

Three trees in one

The structures inside your lungs resemble three upside-down trees. One "tree" is the airway: the trachea branches into smaller bronchi, which divide into bronchioles. Another is the pulmonary artery bringing stale blood from the heart, which divides to form the pulmonary arterioles and finally the alveolar capillaries. The third is the network of pulmonary veins and venules taking refreshed blood back to the heart.

ALVEOLI

The smallest lung airways, the terminal bronchioles, look like tiny twigs of a vine bearing bunches of grapes. The "grapes" are groups of air sacs called alveoli. Around 700 million of them are clustered inside your lungs. Pulmonary arterioles branch and divide to form the smallest blood vessels, the capillaries, which wrap around each alveolus.

Mucous membranes

Elastic fibers

Smooth muscles

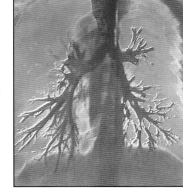

This X-ray shows a rear view of the chest. The bronchial tree branches out in the chest cavity, encased by the ribs.

Mucous membranes

Lining the respiratory system are mucous membranes, which make sticky mucus to keep the structures within moist. Mucus also helps trap dust.

A quick exchange

The alveoli increase the surface area of the lung, so that exchanging oxygen and carbon dioxide is quick and efficient. If all the alveoli were spread flat, they would cover an area nearly the size of a tennis court.

Yawning

When you open your mouth wide in a deep yawn, air rushes into your lungs, expanding the alveoli. No one is quite sure what triggers the yawning reflex, but it usually follows a period of shallow breathing, when you are tired or stressed.

Macrophages

These tiny scavenger cells inside the alveolus "eat" and destroy any dust particles or bacteria that manage to reach your lungs.

INSIDE AN ALVEOLUS

The lining of the alveoli is made of a single layer of thin, flat, curved cells. The walls of the capillaries meshed around the alveoli have a similar construction. As a result, air inside the alveolus is extremely close to the blood cells in the capillary. This means the oxygen in your lungs has the minimum distance to travel in order to enter the bloodstream.

Cells forming alveolar wall

Cells forming capillary wall

Fibrous supporting tissue

Macrophage

Capillary

Hiccups

Sometimes you get hiccups when you eat too quickly. This reflex action happens in two stages. First, the diaphragm contracts sharply when its nerves become irritated. Then, as soon as you breathe in, your larynx snaps shut, making a clicking sound.

Diaphragm

Your diaphragm contracts involuntarily, or without your conscious control. Signals from the brain stimulate its movement.

LEFT JUGULAR VEIN

SUBCLAVIAN VEIN

CAPILLARY NETWORK

ALVEOLI

UPPER LOBE

LEFT PULMONARY ARTERY

ARTERY

BRONCHUS

VEIN

IUM

LOWER LOBE

DIAPHRAGM

ARTERIOLE

VENULE

ALVEOLUS

ALVEOLUS

ALVEOLUS

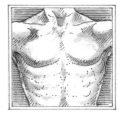

The Heart and Main Blood Vessels

Nestled between the lower parts of your lungs is the heart, a fist-sized bag of muscle. Consisting of two pumps, it contracts and squeezes out its contents more than once every second. It works every minute of every day, never stopping until you die. Your life depends on your heart pumping blood around the 90,000-mile (150,000-km) network of blood vessels.

A wall called the septum separates the two pumps in the heart. The pump on the left side (shown on the right in the pictures) squirts bright red, oxygen-rich blood into the main artery, the aorta. This leads into a network of blood vessels that reaches every part of your body. The blood passes on its oxygen to the body tissues and oozes back, dark reddish purple, along veins into the right side of the heart. From there it is pumped out to the lungs, where it is refreshed with new oxygen. This turns the blood bright red again. It returns to the left pump and into the aorta, to complete its figure-eight circuit.

CORONARY VESSELS

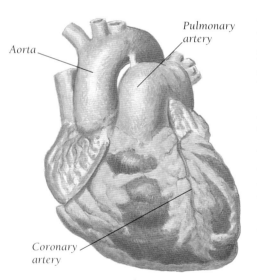

Aorta

Pulmonary artery

Coronary artery

Like all body organs, your heart needs a supply of blood to bring it oxygen. It cannot get oxygen from the blood within its chambers, which passes through too quickly and under too great pressure, and in the right pump is very low in oxygen. So the muscle that makes up the wall of the heart, called the myocardium, receives oxygen-rich blood from a system of small arteries that branch from the aorta. These are called coronary arteries. They snake over the heart's surface, dividing and sending tiny branches into the heart muscle.

HOW VALVES WORK

A series of valves ensures that blood flows only one way. At the two exits leading from the heart into the main arteries, are crescent-shaped valves. A valve shaped like a half-moon sits at each of the two exits leading from the heart into the main arteries. When the heart refills, they balloon out, sealed along their edges to prevent the blood from flowing backward.

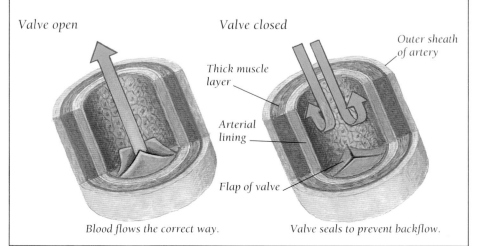

Valve open

Valve closed

Outer sheath of artery

Thick muscle layer

Arterial lining

Flap of valve

Blood flows the correct way.

Valve seals to prevent backflow.

Superior vena cava

This main vein carries used blood from the head, arms, and upper body back to the heart. The inferior vena cava, which enters the heart from beneath, returns blood from the lower body and legs.

Right coronary artery

No wider than a drinking straw, this coronary artery loops around the lower side and to the rear of the heart. It supplies blood to the thick muscle of the lower pumping chamber, the right ventricle. On the other side, the left coronary artery does the same for the left ventricle.

Pulmonary arteries

The two pulmonary arteries, which bring blood to the lungs for replenishment, are the only arteries in the body that carry dark, low-oxygen blood.

Blood passes easily through the smooth vessel lining.

Flexible muscle and tissue withstand blood pressure.

Atrium and ventricle

The heart consists of four chambers, the right atrium and right ventricle (which together form the right pump) and the left atrium and left ventricle (the left pump). The atria receive blood from the veins and pass it into the ventricles. The ventricles pump the blood into the arteries, which leave the heart.

Tricuspid valve

A three-pointed valve between the right atrium and right ventricle prevents blood from surging back into the atrium as the ventricle contracts powerfully. Its thin anchoring tendons keep it from turning inside out.

Interventricular septum

This dividing wall is slightly off-center. That means the left ventricle – the one with the greater job of pumping blood all around the body – is larger and more muscular than the right ventricle.

SUPERIOR VENA CAVA

RIGHT PULMONARY ARTERY

FAT

MUSCLE

LEFT CORONARY ARTERY

RIGHT CORONARY ARTERY

RIGHT PULMONARY VEIN

RIGHT PULMONARY VEIN

RIGHT CORONARY NERVES

MYOCA

TRIC

INFERIOR VENA CAVA

Aortic arch

The body's biggest blood vessel, the aorta, arches out of the heart and down toward the lower body. It has an internal diameter of about 1 in. (25 mm), and blood gushes through it at a speed of about 8 in. (20 cm) per second.

Coronary nerves

Nerves stimulate the constantly pumping heart muscle. They pass on signals from the brain, which continually monitors the needs of the body. These signals tell the heart how fast it should pump to meet the body's demands.

This shrivelled vessel is the remnant of a bypass tube, the ductus arteriosus. Your lungs did not work before birth, so this tube shunted blood meant for the lungs into the aorta. After birth, it shrank and sealed itself.

HEARTBEAT CYCLE

There are four phases to every heartbeat. The relax-and-refilling (phases 1 and 2 below) is called diastole. The contract-and-squeeze pumping (phases 3 and 4) is known as systole. The whole cycle lasts, on average, only four-fifths of a second. The four phases of the beat merge into one sequence and run smoothly into the next beat.

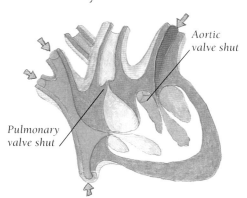

Phase 1: The atria relax and blood flows into them from the main veins.

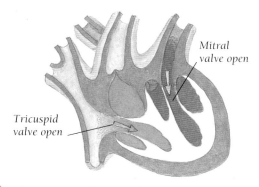

Phase 2: Blood passes from the atria, through the tricuspid and mitral valves, to the ventricles below.

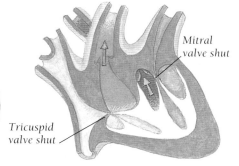

Phase 3: The ventricles contract and force blood through the aortic and pulmonary valves into the main arteries.

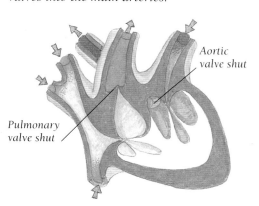

Phase 4: The ventricles have each ejected 5 Tbs. (70 ml) of blood. They relax as the cycle begins again.

Pericardium

A thin, slippery bag, called the pericardium, wraps around the heart, enclosing a layer of fluid. This and the fatty pads lubricate the pulsing heart's squirming motions.

Mitral valve

This structure, situated between the left atrium and ventricle, permits blood to go one way only. The long chordae tendineae help stop it from flipping inside out.

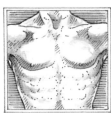

The Upper Back

HOLD YOUR ARMS STRAIGHT out sideways.
Feel the muscles tensing in your upper arms and
shoulders, and in your back, especially between your scapulae
(shoulder blades). Before long, you will begin to feel how heavy your
arms and hands are, with their many muscles and bones, blood vessels,
and nerves. The broad intertwined muscles in your upper back and
shoulders, shown here, must be strong enough to lift and move your arms
and hands – plus any heavy objects you are holding!

Next, stretch both of your arms straight up in the air. Then hold them straight
out in front of you, palms together; swing them back horizontally, as far as you
can; lower them behind you; and, finally, let them hang by your sides. This
demonstrates the wide range of movements made possible by your shoulders.
The shoulder is among the body's most mobile, flexible joints, and the
reasons why are illustrated at the bottom of the page. Your shoulders enable
your arms to reach out in almost any direction, even behind your back –
with a little help from bent elbows!

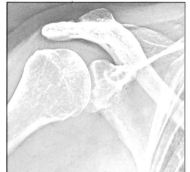

The three bones that meet at the
shoulder joint are seen in this
X-ray: the scapula (shoulder
blade), clavicle (collarbone),
and humerus.

A LOOK BACK
Providing the framework for the powerful
muscles of the upper back are the rib cage,
the scapulae, and the shoulder joints. Most
joints are stable because the bones fit
together snugly, held by ligaments. But in
the shoulder, stability lies mainly in
the six muscles immediately around
the bones: the deltoid, supraspinatus,
infraspinatus, teres major, teres
minor, and subscapularis.

Under wraps
Smooth, glistening cartilage covers
the ends of the humerus and scapula
inside the joint to reduce friction as
the joint moves. A tough capsule of
ropelike ligaments surrounds the
joint membranes.

THE SHOULDER JOINT
This is a ball-and-socket joint.
The ball is the rounded top, or head,
of the humerus bone, and the
socket is a hollow in the
scapula, called the glenoid
cavity. To allow the widest
range of movement, the socket is
not as deep as the one in your hip
bone. That is why the shoulder is
more easily dislocated, or "put out of
joint," under stress.

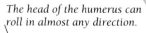

The head of the humerus can
roll in almost any direction.

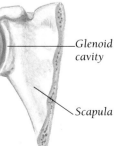

Glenoid
cavity

Scapula

Humerus

Shoulder holders
The supraspinatus, infraspinatus, and
teres minor muscles help support and
protect the shoulder joint, keeping the
head of the humerus bone in place.

SEMISPINALIS CAPITIS

SPLENIUS CAPITIS

TRAPEZIUS

FIRST

SECOND RIB

THIRD

SUPRASPINATUS

ACROMION

SCAPULA

SEMISPINALIS

INFRASPINATUS

ARTERY OF SCAPULA

SUPRA SPINATUS

INFRA SPINATUS

TERES MINOR

JOINT CAPSULE

HEAD OF HUMERUS

GLENOID CAVITY

BICEPS

DELTOID

HUMERUS

TERES MAJOR

TRICEPS (LONG HEAD)

TERES MINOR

EIGHTH

NINTH RIB

TERES MAJOR

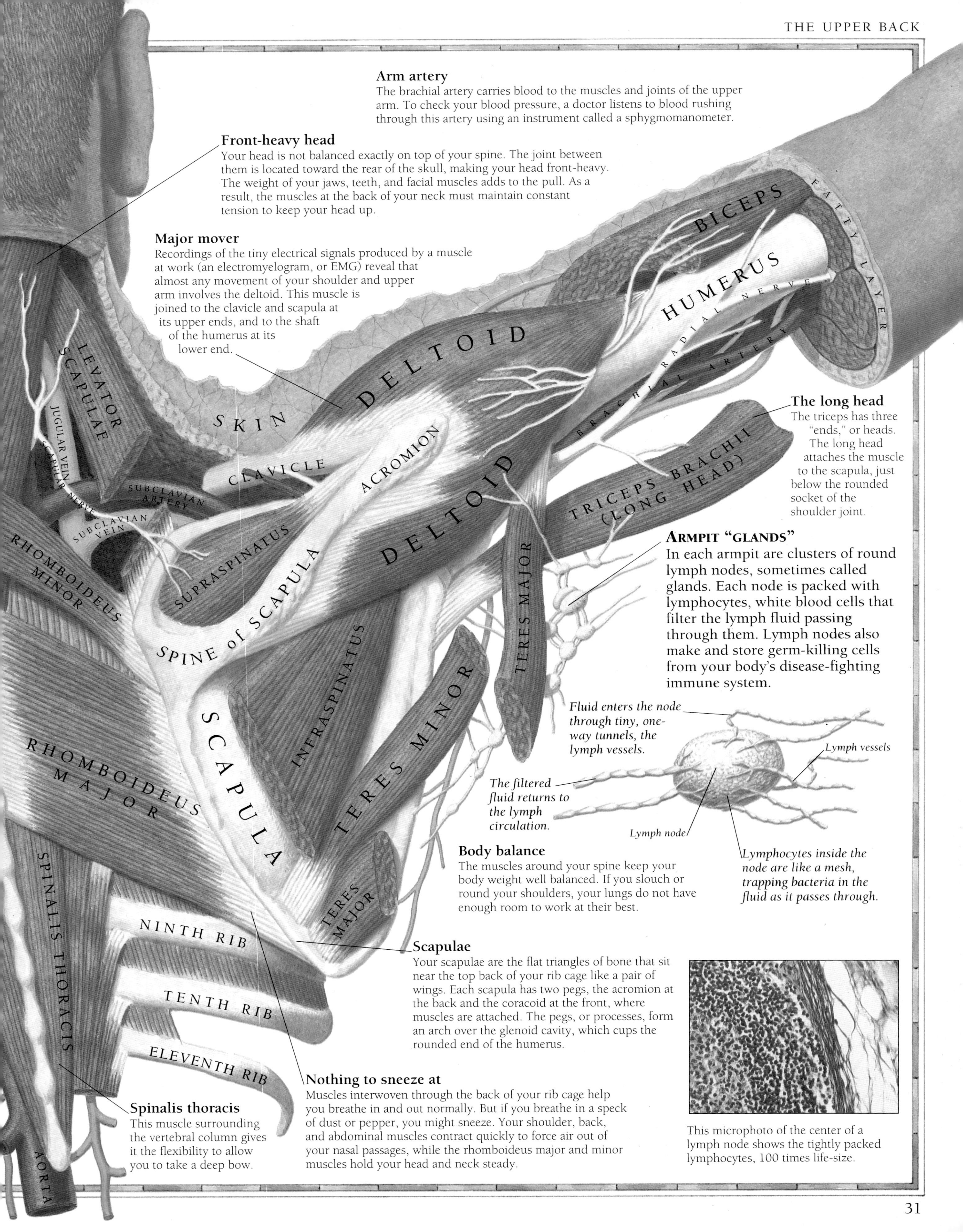

Arm artery
The brachial artery carries blood to the muscles and joints of the upper arm. To check your blood pressure, a doctor listens to blood rushing through this artery using an instrument called a sphygmomanometer.

Front-heavy head
Your head is not balanced exactly on top of your spine. The joint between them is located toward the rear of the skull, making your head front-heavy. The weight of your jaws, teeth, and facial muscles adds to the pull. As a result, the muscles at the back of your neck must maintain constant tension to keep your head up.

Major mover
Recordings of the tiny electrical signals produced by a muscle at work (an electromyelogram, or EMG) reveal that almost any movement of your shoulder and upper arm involves the deltoid. This muscle is joined to the clavicle and scapula at its upper ends, and to the shaft of the humerus at its lower end.

The long head
The triceps has three "ends," or heads. The long head attaches the muscle to the scapula, just below the rounded socket of the shoulder joint.

ARMPIT "GLANDS"
In each armpit are clusters of round lymph nodes, sometimes called glands. Each node is packed with lymphocytes, white blood cells that filter the lymph fluid passing through them. Lymph nodes also make and store germ-killing cells from your body's disease-fighting immune system.

Fluid enters the node through tiny, one-way tunnels, the lymph vessels.

Lymph vessels

The filtered fluid returns to the lymph circulation.

Lymph node

Lymphocytes inside the node are like a mesh, trapping bacteria in the fluid as it passes through.

Body balance
The muscles around your spine keep your body weight well balanced. If you slouch or round your shoulders, your lungs do not have enough room to work at their best.

Scapulae
Your scapulae are the flat triangles of bone that sit near the top back of your rib cage like a pair of wings. Each scapula has two pegs, the acromion at the back and the coracoid at the front, where muscles are attached. The pegs, or processes, form an arch over the glenoid cavity, which cups the rounded end of the humerus.

Nothing to sneeze at
Muscles interwoven through the back of your rib cage help you breathe in and out normally. But if you breathe in a speck of dust or pepper, you might sneeze. Your shoulder, back, and abdominal muscles contract quickly to force air out of your nasal passages, while the rhomboideus major and minor muscles hold your head and neck steady.

Spinalis thoracis
This muscle surrounding the vertebral column gives it the flexibility to allow you to take a deep bow.

Labels on illustration:
BICEPS · HUMERUS · FATTY LAYER · RADIAL NERVE · BRACHIAL ARTERY · TRICEPS BRACHII (LONG HEAD) · TERES MAJOR · DELTOID · SKIN · CLAVICLE · ACROMION · SPINE of SCAPULA · SUPRASPINATUS · INFRASPINATUS · TERES MINOR · TERES MAJOR · SCAPULA · RHOMBOIDEUS MAJOR · RHOMBOIDEUS MINOR · LEVATOR SCAPULAE · JUGULAR VEIN · SCAPULAR VEIN · SUBCLAVIAN NERVE · SUBCLAVIAN ARTERY · SUBCLAVIAN VEIN · SPINALIS THORACIS · NINTH RIB · TENTH RIB · ELEVENTH RIB · AORTA

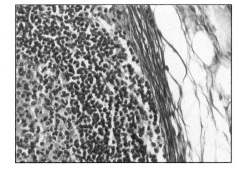

This microphoto of the center of a lymph node shows the tightly packed lymphocytes, 100 times life-size.

The Spinal Column

RUNNING DOWN THE MIDDLE OF YOUR BACK is the spine, a vital supporting rod for your head and body. The spine, also known as the spinal column or backbone, is a flexible chain of closely linked bones. These bones, called vertebrae, are linked by joints that allow slight movement with the bones above and below them. Over the entire length of the spine, however, these many small movements add up. Your spine lets you twist your upper body around, touch your toes, and turn a somersault.

The spinal column houses the spinal cord. This thick bundle of nerves transmits information back and forth between your brain and the rest of your body. It merges with the brain in the base of the skull and extends partway down the inside of the spine through a tunnel consisting of holes within the vertebrae. Muscles, blood vessels, and nerves sit at the front and sides of the spine.

Side view

Seen from the side, the spine has a gentle S-shaped curve, bending toward the rear in the neck and upper chest and toward the front in the lower back. You have 24 individual vertebrae, of three main kinds: 7 neck (cervical) vertebrae, 12 chest (thoracic) vertebrae, and 5 lower back (lumbar) vertebrae. Below these are the triangular sacrum and the taillike coccyx.

Curved spine

Your spine has three main curves that help balance the weight of your upper body evenly over your legs and feet. The cervical curve developed when you learned to hold up your own head as a baby, and the lumbar curve developed when you learned to walk and stand upright.

Cervical vertebrae

Two specialized bones, the atlas and axis, sit on top of the other cervical vertebrae. Side "wings" called transverse processes extend from each vertebra. The vertebral artery runs through holes in these processes. The seventh vertebra has a long backward-pointing hook, the spinous process, which anchors a neck ligament. You can feel it through your skin as a knob at the base of your neck.

Thoracic vertebrae

Each thoracic vertebra in the upper back supports a pair of ribs. Small hollows called facets hold the ribs in place. These bones work with the cervical vertebrae above when you bend over to tie your shoe or bend backward to look up.

Rear view

The parts of your spine that stick out like hooks are called the spinous processes. They act as anchor points for muscles that keep your whole spine tensed and upright. This prevents your front-heavy body from toppling forward! The spinal cord does not continue to the base of your spinal column. It divides into numerous individual nerves at about the level of the first and second lumbar vertebrae.

A supple spine allows this acrobat to bend almost double.

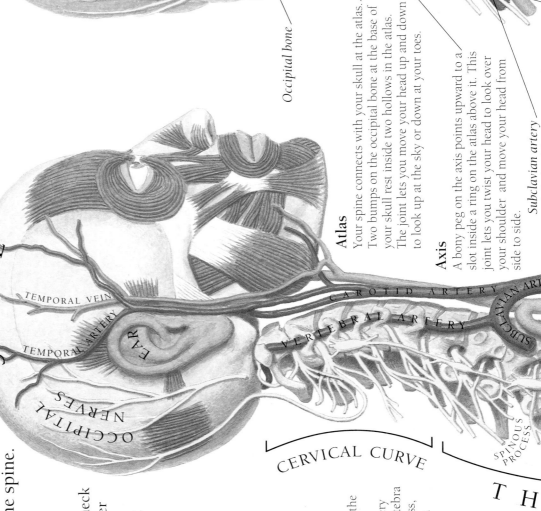

OCCIPITAL NERVES

SKULL

OCCIPITAL NERVES

ATLAS

AXIS

3

4

5

6

SEVENTH CERVICAL

FIRST THORACIC

2

3

4

Right subclavian artery

Subclavian vein from right shoulder

Occipital bone

Left subclavian vein

Atlas
Your spine connects with your skull at the atlas. Two bumps on the occipital bone at the base of your skull rest inside two hollows in the atlas. The joint lets you move your head up and down to look up at the sky or down at your toes.

Axis
A bony peg on the axis points upward to a slot inside a ring on the atlas above it. This joint lets you twist your head to look over your shoulder and move your head from side to side.

Subclavian artery to left shoulder

SKULL

TEMPORAL VEIN

TEMPORAL ARTERY

EAR

OCCIPITAL NERVES

CAROTID ARTERY

VERTEBRAL ARTERY

SUBCLAVIAN ARTERY

CERVICAL CURVE

SPINOUS PROCESS

THO

Nerves pass through four pairs of foramen (holes).

Ligaments join the coccyx to the sacrum.

5 6 7 8 9 10 11 TWELFTH THORACIC FIRST LUMBAR 2 3 4 5 SUPRASPINOUS LIGAMENT COCCYX

SACRUM

SACRUM

Sacral plexus of nerves

Nerve roots
Thirty-one pairs of nerves branch from the spinal cord and pass along shallow grooves between the vertebrae, out to the surrounding organs and tissues. These are the spinal nerve roots.

Arch of aorta

Superior vena cava

Thoracic aorta

Spinal support
The spine is stabilized and supported by ligaments between each pair of vertebrae, and two tough ligaments (infraspinous and supraspinous) running its entire length. Muscles and tendons attached to the spine control its movements and provide added support.

Abdominal aorta
Freshly oxygenated blood squirts out of your heart and into arteries serving your head and arms before pouring down your aorta. At about an inch (25 mm) wide, this is the largest artery in your body. Its name changes as it passes through the body. Here, it is called the abdominal aorta.

Common iliac artery

Common iliac vein

Between the bones
Tough, flexible disks cushion and separate the vertebrae. You are slightly taller in the morning than you are when you go to bed. This is because the disks, which are pressed together all day as you sit and stand, expand to their normal thickness while you sleep.

Sacrum and coccyx
Five vertebrae fuse together to form the triangle-shaped sacrum. It is joined to the bottom lumbar vertebra above, the hip bones on either side, and the coccyx below. The coccyx, or "tailbone," contains four more fused vertebrae.

ABDOMINAL AORTA

INFERIOR VENA CAVA

AZYGOS VEIN

SACRUM

COCCYX

SACRAL CURVE

LUMBAR CURVE

RACIC CURVE

All vertebrates – mammals, amphibians, fish, birds, and reptiles such as this snake – have spines. A snake is almost all spine, with up to 400 vertebrae.

Bony tunnel
The large hole in the middle of each vertebra is called the vertebral foramen. When the vertebrae are stacked on top of each other, the holes line up to form a tunnel for the spinal cord called the vertebral canal.

Azygos vein
This vein runs up the right side of the spinal column to empty into the superior vena cava, draining used blood from the chest along the way. If the inferior vena cava is blocked, blood can travel back to the heart along this bypass route.

Lumbar vertebrae
Your spinal column carries an increasing load toward its base, which is reflected in the larger, stronger lumbar vertebrae in the lower back. These are the bones that take the most stress when you lift a heavy weight. The joint between the fifth lumbar vertebra and the sacrum is often involved in a "slipped disk."

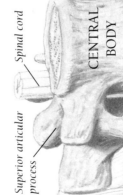

Spinal cord

CENTRAL BODY

DISK

CENTRAL BODY

Nerve roots

Superior articular process

Inferior articular facet

INTERVERTEBRAL JOINT
Between the main parts, or central bodies, of each pair of vertebrae is a tough pad called the intervertebral disk. Each disk has a firm outer layer and a gelatinlike center, the nucleus pulposus. The entire disk absorbs shocks as your move, and withstands squashing as the spinal column bends and twists. The vertebrae link together with two curved bumps, the superior articular processes, which fit into inferior articular facets of the vertebra just above to form a joint. The spinal cord passes through the vertebral canal behind the central bodies.

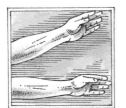

The Arm and Hand

Y OU ARE WALKING THROUGH A GARDEN late at night, guided by the powerful beam from your flashlight. Suddenly, the light fails and you find yourself in pitch darkness. Instinctively, you stretch out your arms in front of you and fan your fingertips, groping for the slightest contact. Your arms and hands are important for their touching and sensing abilities, as well as for their ability to grasp and manipulate.

As you feel your way toward the glow of the distant house, one of your fingers touches a needlelike point. You react almost at once by jerking your hand away. Then your flashlight comes on again, and you can see the point – a prickly thistle. The skin in your fingertip registered the pressure of a thorn; nerve signals flashed the information to your brain, your brain sent out nerve signals to the many muscles in your arm, and these muscles contracted, pulling your hand away from the thistle – all in a split second.

JUGGLING HANDS
As the expert juggler throws and catches, his eyes follow the movements of the balls. Muscles in his arms and hands make them reach out to the exact position where each object will fall. The skin on his hands confirms contact and safe grip of the ball, even as the muscles prepare for the next throw. It is an amazing series of fast, precise movements.

A SENSITIVE TOUCH
Human arms and hands are incredibly flexible. Their complex network of nerves, blood vessels, and muscles makes them among the most efficient manipulating devices in nature. Nerve endings and clusters of sense receptors in the skin, particularly in extra-sensitive areas such as the fingertips, send messages to the brain. Strong tendons joining the muscles to the bones mean that the body can react to these messages very quickly.

The first digit, or finger, is known as the index finger. Index comes from a Latin word meaning "pointer."

Wristbands
About 10 blood vessels and nerves, and more than 20 tendons, pass through the wrist area. These are bound by two fibrous bands just under the skin, which together look like a wide watch strap. The bands are the flexor retinaculum on the palm side (not visible here) and the extensor retinaculum on the back of the wrist, here separated to expose the tendons running under it.

EXTENSOR RETINACULUM

POLLEX (THUMB)

CEPHALIC VEIN

EXTENSOR POLLICIS LONGUS

TENDONS of EXTENSOR DIGITORUM

DORSAL INTEROSSEI MUSCLE

DORSAL VENOUS NETWORK

DORSAL VEIN

ABDUCTOR POLLICIS LONGUS

EXTENSOR CARPI RADIALIS BREVIS

EXTENSOR,

FAT LAYER SKIN

EXTENSOR TENDON

TENDON

DIGITAL VEIN

TENDON

EXTENSOR TENDON

DIGITAL VEIN

FAT LAYER

EXTENSOR TENDON

DIGITAL ARTERY

ABDUCTOR DIGITI MINIMI

ULNAR NERVE

BASILIC VEIN

EXTENSOR CARPI ULNARIS

RADIAL NERVE

ULNA

PHALANX

EXTENSOR TENDON

PHALANX

DIGITAL ARTERY

PHALANX

MINIMUS (PINKY FINGER)

FATTY PAD

Interosseus artery

FLEXOR CARPI ULNARIS

Between the bones
Interosseus means "between bones." The body has several interosseus vessels. This one is an artery between the radius and ulna bones of the forearm.

All in the wrist
This is the muscle you use to bend your hand at the wrist. It gets its name from the carpus (wrist bones) and the ulna (forearm bone).

Backhand vessels
A web of arteries, veins, and nerves covers the back of your hand. There are two sets each of arteries and veins, superficial and deep. The superficial veins are just under the skin and are often visible from the outside as bluish lines. The deep veins run lower, in among the muscles.

A sense of position
Many of the body's muscles and joints have dozens of microscopic, spindle-shaped stretch sensors in them. They detect whether a muscle is pulled tight or hanging loose and whether a joint is bent or straight. This information is fed along nerves to the brain, which can then work out the positions and postures of various parts of the body. That's how you know without looking if your arm is bent or straight, and whether your fingers are curled or spread. This awareness of body position is called the proprioceptive sense.

At your fingertips
A copious supply of nerves collects signals from the many thousands of sense receptors in the skin of the palm and fingers. Under the ridged skin is a layer of fat that squashes like a cushion as you hold things, for comfort and to improve grip.

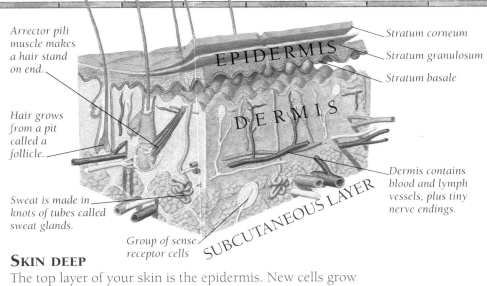

Arrector pili muscle makes a hair stand on end.

EPIDERMIS

Stratum corneum
Stratum granulosum
Stratum basale

DERMIS

Hair grows from a pit called a follicle.

Dermis contains blood and lymph vessels, plus tiny nerve endings.

Sweat is made in knots of tubes called sweat glands.

Group of sense receptor cells

SUBCUTANEOUS LAYER

YOUR SKIN

Your body is protected and covered by its outer layer, the skin. The drawing on the left shows what a section of your skin looks like when magnified about 50 times. Your skin makes up more than one-tenth of your body weight and is made of two parts, the epidermis and the dermis. It protects your internal organs from injury and helps stop invading bacteria and the harmful rays of the sun from reaching them. It also stops the internal body fluids from leaking away and helps keep the inside of the body at a constant temperature. Your skin also contains waxes, oils, and other substances that make it waterproof. Without them, you might soak up your bathwater like a sponge.

SKIN DEEP

The top layer of your skin is the epidermis. New cells grow continually from its lower part, the stratum basale. These cells pass up to the stratum granulosum. There, some cells make the protein keratin, which toughens them. Other cells in the stratum basale produce melanin, the substance that gives skin its color. The stratum granulosum cells fill with keratin and die as they continue upward to reach the top surface, the stratum corneum. After a month or so, the cells are worn away by friction. The dermis, about four times thicker than the epidermis, consists mainly of the protein collagen, which builds scar tissue to mend cuts and abrasions. Underneath it is the fatty subcutaneous layer.

Biceps and triceps

The biceps and triceps muscles control the up and down movements of your forearm. The biceps has two heads, or points of attachment to the bone. The triceps has three heads: long, lateral, and medial. To tell the difference between the biceps muscle in your leg (the biceps femoris muscle), the one in your arm is called the biceps brachii.

The thick, powerful deltoid muscle moves the humerus bone.

DELTOID MUSCLE
BICEPS BRACHII
LONG HEAD
SHORT HEAD
CEPHALIC VEIN
BRACHIALIS
HUMERUS
CIRCUMFLEX ARTERY
SCAPULA
TERES MINOR
TERES MAJOR
RADIAL ARTERY
RADIAL NERVE
TRICEPS LATERAL HEAD
TRICEPS
LONG HEAD
LATISSIMUS DORSI
RIB
RIB
RIB
CEPHALIC VEIN
DIGITORUM
BRACHIORADIALIS
EXTENSOR CARPI RADIALIS LONGUS
ACCESSORY CEPHALIC VEIN
EXTENSOR CARPI ULNARIS
MEDIAN VEIN
ULNA
ANCONEUS
ELBOW
TRICEPS TENDON
TRICEPS LATERAL HEAD
FATTY LAYER
SKIN
SERRATUS ANTERIOR

The arm joints

The series of joints from the shoulder to the fingertips makes your arms extremely flexible. The ball-and-socket joint inside your shoulder lets you move your arm in almost any direction. The hinge joint at your elbow enables you to fold your arm in half and straighten it out again. The joint at the junction of the wrist bones gives flexibility to your hand. You can bend and stretch your fingers because of the hinge joints inside them.

HAND TOUCH MAP

The skin on the palms of your hands – especially on your fingertips – is richly supplied with sense receptors that provide your sense of touch. On the back of your hand, as in many parts of the body, these receptors are wrapped around the base of each hair, so that they can sense any movement of the hair shaft. In hairless areas like the palms, lips, and tongue, the cells are thickly clustered in disks within the skin.

The darker the shading, the more sensitive the area.

Less sensitive   More sensitive

A bypass for blood

Just above the elbow, the chief forearm vessels, the radial and ulnar arteries, join to form the brachial artery. This is the main tube bringing fresh blood into the arm. It has several smaller branches that divide and join again to create a network of bypasses, or "short cuts," for the blood. This type of system is called collateral circulation. Blood can get through it by a number of collateral (running "side by side") routes.

The Shoulder and Elbow

Pretend you've won. Raise your clenched fist in a salute of triumph. You are using many of the powerful muscles in your shoulder and upper arm shown here. The bulge you see under the skin of your upper arm is the biceps brachii muscle. Like other muscles, the biceps bulges in the middle as it shortens. This type of muscle action is called isotonic contraction. The muscle keeps the same tone, or pulling power, but shortens as the elbow bends. Now clench your fist and tense your biceps to "make a muscle," but keep your arm still. The biceps still bulges. This is isometric contraction: The muscle exerts more pulling power, but stays the same length. Most muscles undergo a combination of isometric and isotonic contractions, as they move or hold steady the parts of your body.

Biceps and triceps muscles work together to stabilize the arm.

A gymnast working on the parallel bars can support his or her entire body weight using the muscles of the upper arm and shoulder.

THE SHOULDER AND UPPER ARM

Whether you are lifting a heavy weight or picking up a feather, the muscles in your upper arm and shoulder provide both power and accuracy. Muscles in the upper back and shoulder move the upper arm; muscles in the upper arm move the forearm; and muscles in the forearm move the wrist and hand. The whole arm is a three-section lever. With it, you can reach out and grasp an apple, then fold your arm back on itself to raise the apple to your mouth.

THE "DOUBLE-JOINTED" SHOULDER

Your shoulder is a very flexible ball-and-socket joint. A significant factor in its mobility is the movement of the scapula (shoulder blade). The scapula's movements alter the angle of the socket, which cradles the ball at the upper end of the humerus (upper arm bone). When you raise your arm through a half circle (180°) – from hanging at your side to straight above your head – about half of the movement is due to the scapula shifting its position.

More than 180° of movement in vertical plane at side of body

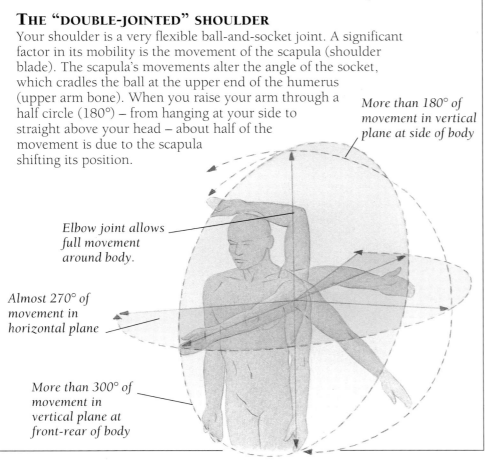

Elbow joint allows full movement around body.

Almost 270° of movement in horizontal plane

More than 300° of movement in vertical plane at front-rear of body

Pectoralis pairs

Under the thick triangular slab of the pectoralis major, the main chest muscle, is the smaller pectoralis minor. It links the third, fourth, and fifth ribs with the scapula and the humerus. When it contracts, it pulls the scapula around to the side of the rib cage. This allows your arm to swing across your chest, so that your fingers can touch the opposite shoulder.

Rib muscles

Thin sheets of muscle called the intercostals weave between the bones of your rib cage. Nerves and blood vessels also fill the space between the ribs.

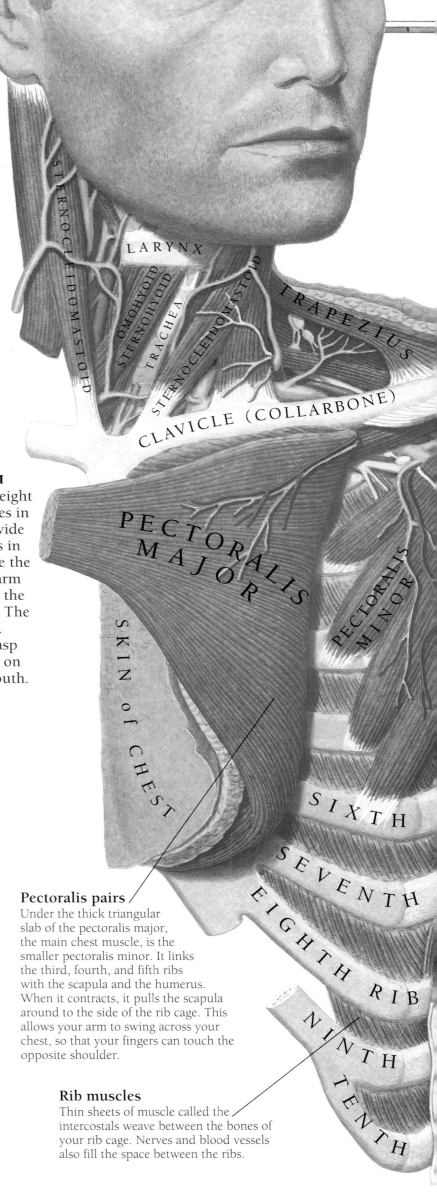

STERNOCLEIDOMASTOID
LARYNX
OMOHYOID
STERNOHYOID
TRACHEA
STERNOCLEIDOMASTOID
TRAPEZIUS
CLAVICLE (COLLARBONE)
PECTORALIS MAJOR
PECTORALIS MINOR
SKIN OF CHEST
SIXTH
SEVENTH
EIGHTH RIB
NINTH
TENTH

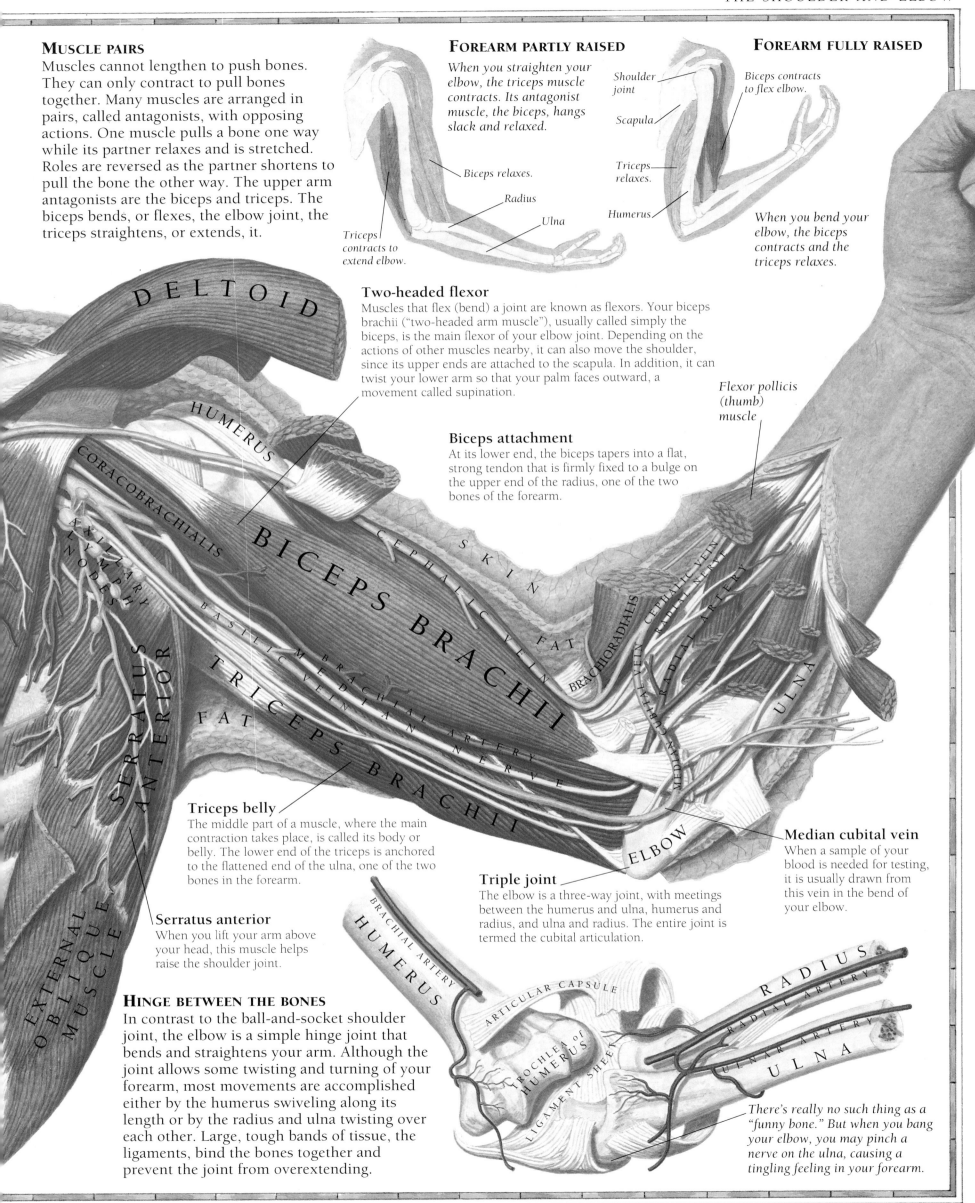

MUSCLE PAIRS

Muscles cannot lengthen to push bones. They can only contract to pull bones together. Many muscles are arranged in pairs, called antagonists, with opposing actions. One muscle pulls a bone one way while its partner relaxes and is stretched. Roles are reversed as the partner shortens to pull the bone the other way. The upper arm antagonists are the biceps and triceps. The biceps bends, or flexes, the elbow joint, the triceps straightens, or extends, it.

FOREARM PARTLY RAISED

When you straighten your elbow, the triceps muscle contracts. Its antagonist muscle, the biceps, hangs slack and relaxed.

Biceps relaxes.

Radius

Ulna

Triceps contracts to extend elbow.

FOREARM FULLY RAISED

Biceps contracts to flex elbow.

Shoulder joint

Scapula

Triceps relaxes.

Humerus

When you bend your elbow, the biceps contracts and the triceps relaxes.

Two-headed flexor

Muscles that flex (bend) a joint are known as flexors. Your biceps brachii ("two-headed arm muscle"), usually called simply the biceps, is the main flexor of your elbow joint. Depending on the actions of other muscles nearby, it can also move the shoulder, since its upper ends are attached to the scapula. In addition, it can twist your lower arm so that your palm faces outward, a movement called supination.

Biceps attachment

At its lower end, the biceps tapers into a flat, strong tendon that is firmly fixed to a bulge on the upper end of the radius, one of the two bones of the forearm.

Flexor pollicis (thumb) muscle

DELTOID

HUMERUS

CORACOBRACHIALIS

AXILLARY LYMPH NODES

BICEPS BRACHII

SKIN

FAT

CEPHALIC VEIN

BASILIC VEIN

BRACHIAL ARTERY

MEDIAN NERVE

TRICEPS BRACHII

FAT

SERRATUS ANTERIOR

EXTERNAL OBLIQUE MUSCLE

BRACHIORADIALIS

CEPHALIC VEIN

RADIAL NERVE

RADIAL ARTERY

MEDIAN CUBITAL VEIN

ULNA

ELBOW

Triceps belly

The middle part of a muscle, where the main contraction takes place, is called its body or belly. The lower end of the triceps is anchored to the flattened end of the ulna, one of the two bones in the forearm.

Serratus anterior

When you lift your arm above your head, this muscle helps raise the shoulder joint.

Triple joint

The elbow is a three-way joint, with meetings between the humerus and ulna, humerus and radius, and ulna and radius. The entire joint is termed the cubital articulation.

Median cubital vein

When a sample of your blood is needed for testing, it is usually drawn from this vein in the bend of your elbow.

HINGE BETWEEN THE BONES

In contrast to the ball-and-socket shoulder joint, the elbow is a simple hinge joint that bends and straightens your arm. Although the joint allows some twisting and turning of your forearm, most movements are accomplished either by the humerus swiveling along its length or by the radius and ulna twisting over each other. Large, tough bands of tissue, the ligaments, bind the bones together and prevent the joint from overextending.

BRACHIAL ARTERY

HUMERUS

ARTICULAR CAPSULE

TROCHLEA of HUMERUS

LIGAMENT SHEATH

RADIUS

RADIAL ARTERY

ULNAR ARTERY

ULNA

There's really no such thing as a "funny bone." But when you bang your elbow, you may pinch a nerve on the ulna, causing a tingling feeling in your forearm.

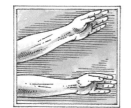

The Wrist, Hand, and Fingers

YOUR HANDS LET YOU "TALK" without speaking: a wave says good-bye, a handshake signals friendship, a gentle caress conveys caring, and a fist punch does the opposite! Your hands are sensitive enough to pass thread through a needle's eye, yet strong enough to squeeze and crush. Of course, many of these abilities depend not only on the structures of your hands, but on your brain, which controls them through your nervous system, and on your eyes and other senses, which provide the necessary information for your brain.

Each hand is built around a skeletal framework of 27 bones connected by a multitude of complex joints that allow amazing flexibility. Wrapped around the bones are muscles and their tendons, blood vessels, nerves – and very little else. Enclosing them all is a layer of skin that contains some of the most sensitive areas in your body, especially on your fingertips. This skin also bears a ridged pattern of swirls and whorls that makes you unique among the more than 5 billion humans on Earth – your fingerprints.

Mechanical hand

Engineers have tried for many years to build a robot that can mimic the human hand. But its movements are too complicated to copy exactly, especially without detailed feedback from touch-sensitive skin and a pair of eyes. Robot hands are used in factory production lines. Although human hands can paint, weld, drill, screw, adjust, and assemble, a separate robot hand-and-arm design is needed for each of these tasks.

BONES OF THE HAND

Your hand has three main anatomical regions. These are the carpus, or wrist, the metacarpus, or palm, and the digits, or fingers. The carpus has eight bones, in two rows of four. Four of these bones link with the radius and ulna bones. Five metacarpal bones stretch from your wrist to your knuckles, and fourteen phalangeal bones shape your fingers. About 40 ligaments, most of them in the wrist, strap the bones together.

Three individually controlled "fingers" give this robot its grip.

A chart from the sixteenth century shows lines and other features interpreted by a palmist.

READING THE LINES

Like fingerprints, the pattern of creases and lines in the skin of the palm is different for each person. Some people believe that the palm pattern reveals the history, health, and fate of the owner. Interpreting creases and lines is called chiromancy, or palmistry. Some palmists also gain a wider impression of the person by chirognomy, studying the hand's overall shape, color, texture, and flexibility.

IN THE PALM OF YOUR HAND

In the view on the right, the skin of the palm is peeled back to reveal the structures that make your hand so flexible. From the thumb (or pollex, meaning "strong") to the pinky finger (or minimus, Latin for "least"), the finger bones are crossed by tendons wrapped in long sheaths. The tendons link the bones to strong muscles in the forearm that control most finger movements. The muscles attached to the metacarpal bones in the palm provide more pulling power, and also give shape to your hand. Blood reaches right up to your fingertips along branches of the radial and ulnar arteries. The entire area is well-supplied with nerve endings linked to the radial, ulnar, and median nerves.

GRIPPING STUFF

From picking up a pin to lifting a heavy suitcase, your hand is well-designed for gripping objects. Three types of grip demonstrate the dexterity of the human hand. The precision grip allows you to hold an object delicately between forefinger and thumb. No other animal, not even our close cousins, chimps and gorillas, have this grip. The thumb can also be tilted to touch, or oppose, the other fingertips. You can mold your fingers and palm around an object with a spherical grip, giving you a secure hold. The power grip of two hands can be strong enough to hold the body's entire weight – imagine hanging onto a chin-up bar.

A precision grip allows highly coordinated work, but does not provide a secure hold.

The first digit, better known as the thumb, has two phalangeal (of the phalanx) bones. The other four digits have three phalangeal bones each.

The ligaments in your wrist keep bones and tendons in place.

RADIUS

ULNA

CARPAL LIGAMENTS

FIRST METACARPAL

SECOND METACARPAL

THIRD METACARPAL

FOURTH METACARPAL

FIFTH METACARPAL

METACARPAL LIGAMENT

PHALANX

Five metacarpal bones of your palm fan out to link with the phalangeal bones of your fingers.

Your finger joints are commonly called knuckles.

A spherical grip is used when holding a round object. The width of the palm gives stability.

In a power grip, the fingers wrap around the object held, with added pressure from the thumb.

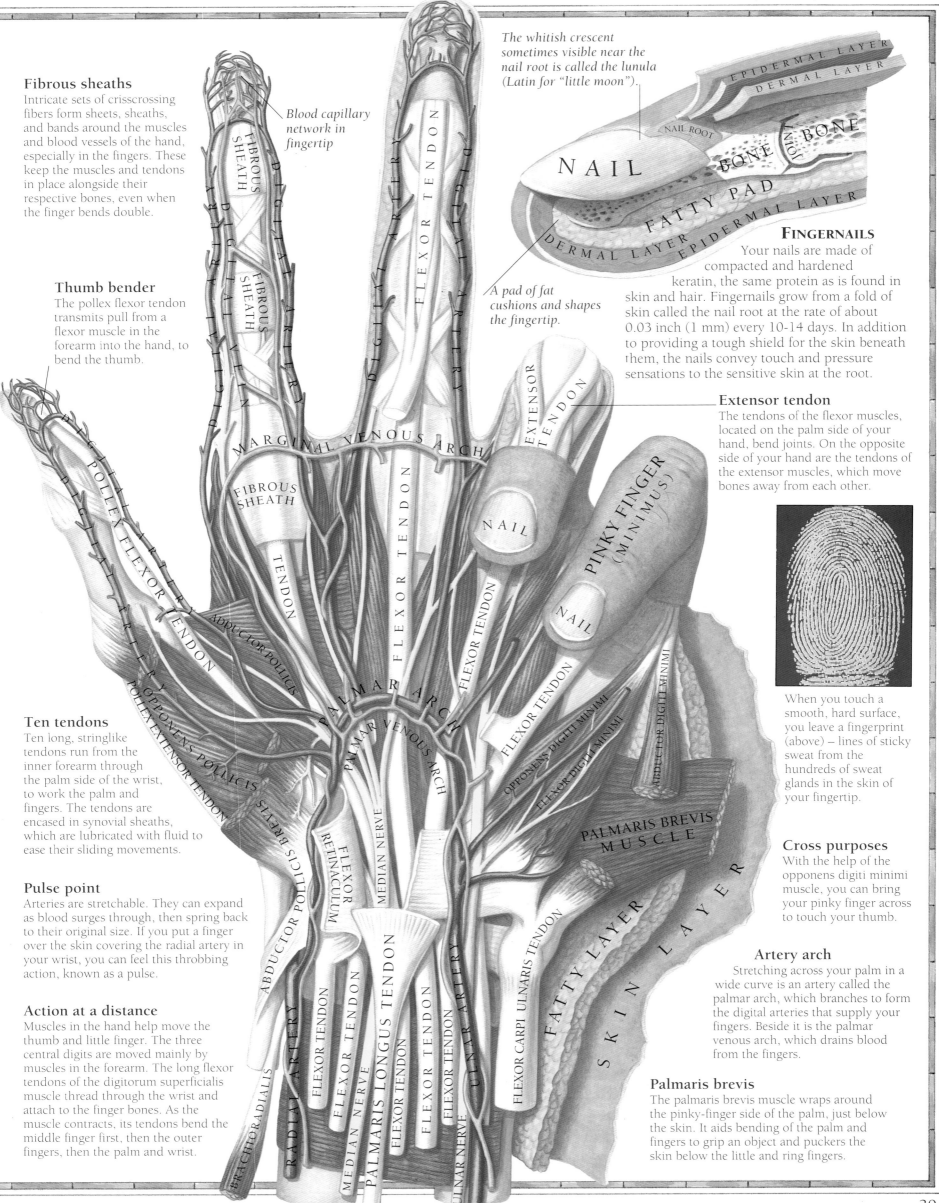

Fibrous sheaths
Intricate sets of crisscrossing fibers form sheets, sheaths, and bands around the muscles and blood vessels of the hand, especially in the fingers. These keep the muscles and tendons in place alongside their respective bones, even when the finger bends double.

Blood capillary network in fingertip

Thumb bender
The pollex flexor tendon transmits pull from a flexor muscle in the forearm into the hand, to bend the thumb.

The whitish crescent sometimes visible near the nail root is called the lunula (Latin for "little moon").

A pad of fat cushions and shapes the fingertip.

FINGERNAILS
Your nails are made of compacted and hardened keratin, the same protein as is found in skin and hair. Fingernails grow from a fold of skin called the nail root at the rate of about 0.03 inch (1 mm) every 10-14 days. In addition to providing a tough shield for the skin beneath them, the nails convey touch and pressure sensations to the sensitive skin at the root.

Extensor tendon
The tendons of the flexor muscles, located on the palm side of your hand, bend joints. On the opposite side of your hand are the tendons of the extensor muscles, which move bones away from each other.

Ten tendons
Ten long, stringlike tendons run from the inner forearm through the palm side of the wrist, to work the palm and fingers. The tendons are encased in synovial sheaths, which are lubricated with fluid to ease their sliding movements.

Pulse point
Arteries are stretchable. They can expand as blood surges through, then spring back to their original size. If you put a finger over the skin covering the radial artery in your wrist, you can feel this throbbing action, known as a pulse.

Action at a distance
Muscles in the hand help move the thumb and little finger. The three central digits are moved mainly by muscles in the forearm. The long flexor tendons of the digitorum superficialis muscle thread through the wrist and attach to the finger bones. As the muscle contracts, its tendons bend the middle finger first, then the outer fingers, then the palm and wrist.

When you touch a smooth, hard surface, you leave a fingerprint (above) – lines of sticky sweat from the hundreds of sweat glands in the skin of your fingertip.

Cross purposes
With the help of the opponens digiti minimi muscle, you can bring your pinky finger across to touch your thumb.

Artery arch
Stretching across your palm in a wide curve is an artery called the palmar arch, which branches to form the digital arteries that supply your fingers. Beside it is the palmar venous arch, which drains blood from the fingers.

Palmaris brevis
The palmaris brevis muscle wraps around the pinky-finger side of the palm, just below the skin. It aids bending of the palm and fingers to grip an object and puckers the skin below the little and ring fingers.

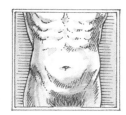

The Lower Torso

YOUR LOWER TORSO is packed with machinery for metabolism, the name for the thousands of chemical processes in the body. The digestive system, consisting mainly of stomach and intestines, takes up most of the space in your abdomen. These organs tunnel through your torso, digesting and absorbing energy- and nutrient-rich substances for growth and repair. Although food is inside your body once you swallow it, it is not truly a part of your body until it is absorbed through the lining of your intestines and into your body tissues.

Your liver, wedged into the top of the lower torso, is like a chemical factory, carrying out hundreds of tasks within its two sections, or lobes. The bottom of your lower torso contains two exits for wastes. Your digestive system expels undigested food and other leftovers from the intestines by way of the anus; your urinary system gets rid of wastes filtered from your blood by way of the urethra.

A MAZE OF TUBES

Compare the picture below with the large one on the right. Moving the intestines outward and slightly to the side exposes the intricate network of arteries and veins supplying blood to the abdominal organs. Normally, these are hidden by the coils of the small and large intestines in front. Behind this maze of piping, just visible against the rear of the abdominal wall, sit the kidneys.

MAIN ORGANS OF THE ABDOMEN

If you peeled away the skin and fat overlying the abdomen, you would see how the organs are coiled, curled, and packed inside, forming a compact conveyor belt for metabolism. The abdomen is bounded above by the dome-shaped diaphragm; at the rear by the spine, hipbones, and back muscles; to the sides and front by large muscle-and-fiber sheets in the abdominal wall; and at the base by the pelvis.

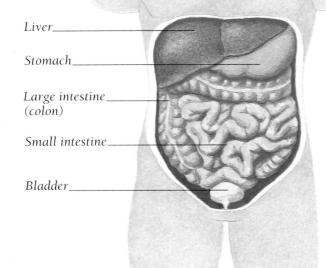

Liver

Stomach

Large intestine (colon)

Small intestine

Bladder

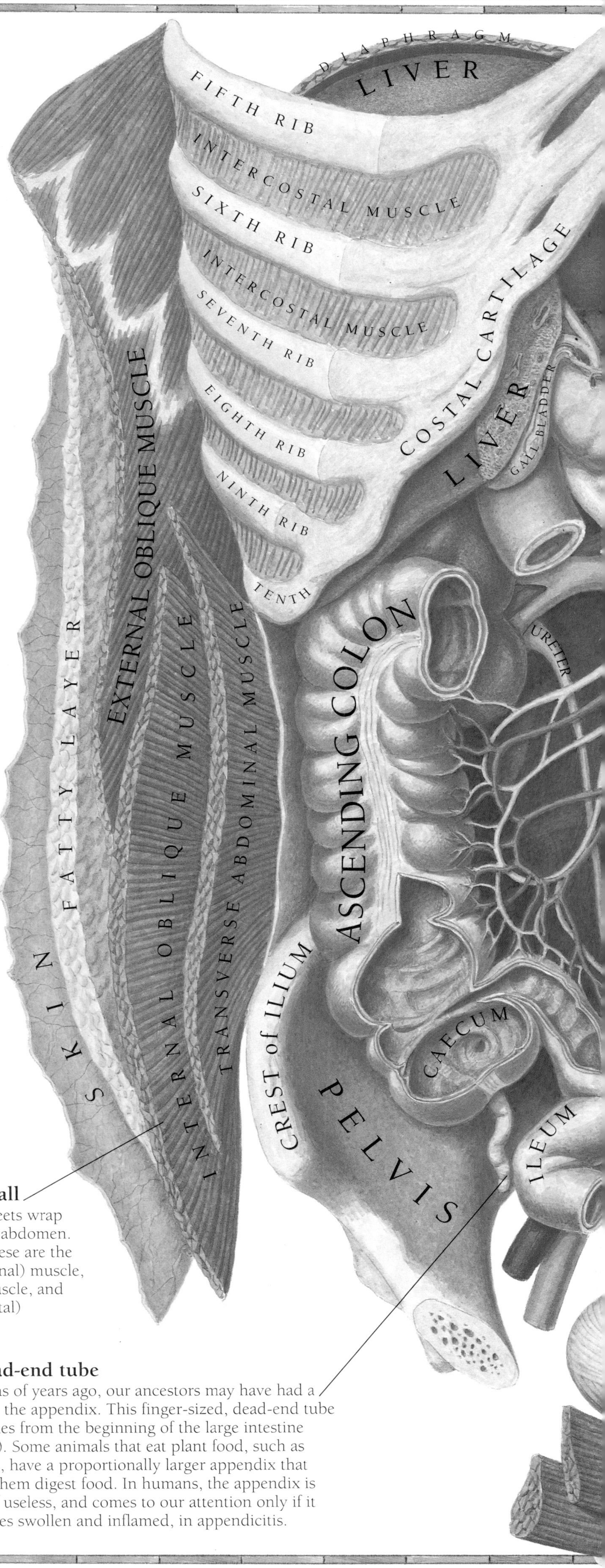

Chest (thorax)

Abdominal side wall
Three broad muscle sheets wrap around the sides of the abdomen. From the outside in, these are the external oblique (diagonal) muscle, the internal oblique muscle, and the transverse (horizontal) abdominal muscle.

A dead-end tube
Millions of years ago, our ancestors may have had a use for the appendix. This finger-sized, dead-end tube branches from the beginning of the large intestine (colon). Some animals that eat plant food, such as rabbits, have a proportionally larger appendix that helps them digest food. In humans, the appendix is largely useless, and comes to our attention only if it becomes swollen and inflamed, in appendicitis.

DIAPHRAGM

LIVER

FIFTH RIB

INTERCOSTAL MUSCLE

SIXTH RIB

INTERCOSTAL MUSCLE

SEVENTH RIB

EIGHTH RIB

NINTH RIB

TENTH

COSTAL CARTILAGE

LIVER

GALL-BLADDER

URETER

EXTERNAL OBLIQUE MUSCLE

INTERNAL OBLIQUE MUSCLE

TRANSVERSE ABDOMINAL MUSCLE

SKIN

FATTY LAYER

CREST of ILIUM

ASCENDING COLON

CAECUM

PELVIS

ILEUM

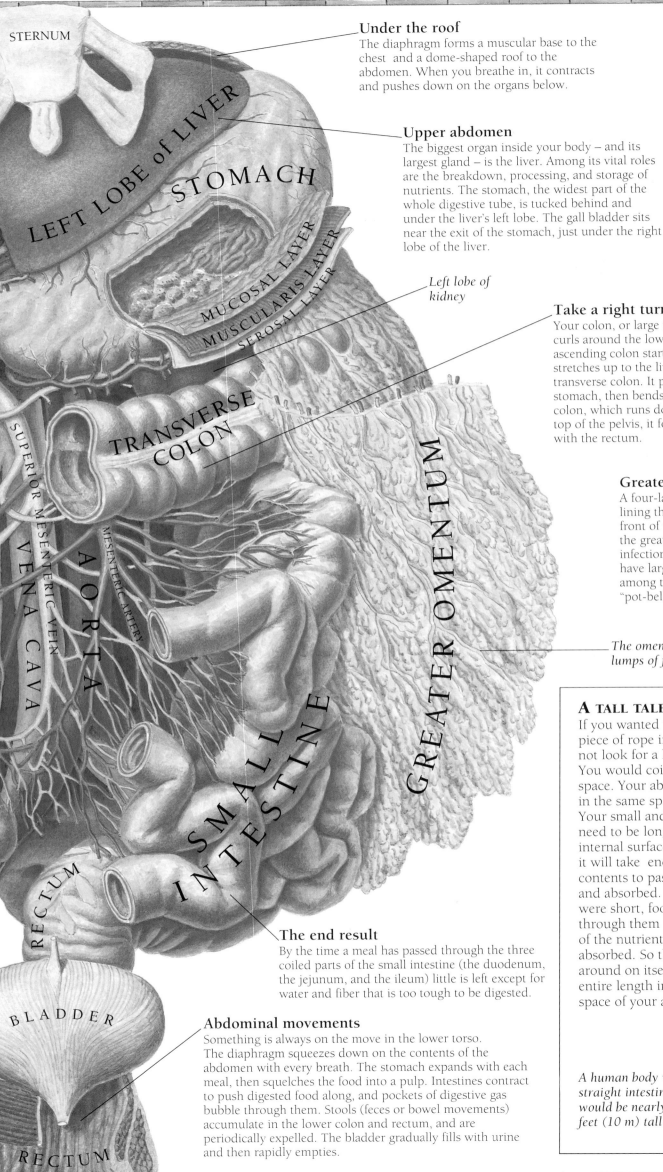

STERNUM

LEFT LOBE of LIVER

STOMACH

MUCOSAL LAYER

MUSCULARIS LAYER

SEROSAL LAYER

SUPERIOR MESENTERIC VEIN

MESENTERIC ARTERY

VENA CAVA

AORTA

TRANSVERSE COLON

GREATER OMENTUM

SMALL INTESTINE

RECTUM

BLADDER

RECTUM

Under the roof

The diaphragm forms a muscular base to the chest and a dome-shaped roof to the abdomen. When you breathe in, it contracts and pushes down on the organs below.

Upper abdomen

The biggest organ inside your body – and its largest gland – is the liver. Among its vital roles are the breakdown, processing, and storage of nutrients. The stomach, the widest part of the whole digestive tube, is tucked behind and under the liver's left lobe. The gall bladder sits near the exit of the stomach, just under the right lobe of the liver.

Left lobe of kidney

Take a right turn at the liver

Your colon, or large intestine, makes an M-shaped loop as it curls around the lower torso. It has four sections. The ascending colon starts at the lower right of the abdomen and stretches up to the liver. There, it bends to the left to form the transverse colon. It passes upward to follow the curve of the stomach, then bends down again to become the descending colon, which runs down the left side of the abdomen. Near the top of the pelvis, it forms the sigmoid colon, curving to connect with the rectum.

Greater omentum

A four-layered fold of peritoneum (the membrane lining the inside of the abdomen) hangs down over the front of the intestines like an apron. This fold, called the greater omentum, contains pads of fat cells and infection-fighting lymph nodes. Some obese people have large lumps of excess fat in the omentum, and among the abdominal organs, which give a "pot-bellied" appearance.

The omentum contains lymph vessels, lumps of fat, and some blood vessels.

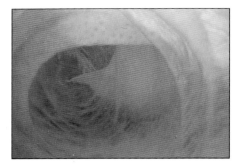

This view of the inner wall of the small intestine was taken with an endoscope, a tubelike instrument for looking into body cavities. Endoscopes can see into the esophagus, stomach, small intestine, large intestine, and bladder.

The end result

By the time a meal has passed through the three coiled parts of the small intestine (the duodenum, the jejunum, and the ileum) little is left except for water and fiber that is too tough to be digested.

Abdominal movements

Something is always on the move in the lower torso. The diaphragm squeezes down on the contents of the abdomen with every breath. The stomach expands with each meal, then squelches the food into a pulp. Intestines contract to push digested food along, and pockets of digestive gas bubble through them. Stools (feces or bowel movements) accumulate in the lower colon and rectum, and are periodically expelled. The bladder gradually fills with urine and then rapidly empties.

A TALL TALE

If you wanted to carry a long piece of rope in a bag, you would not look for a long, thin bag. You would coil the rope to save space. Your abdomen is designed in the same space-saving way. Your small and large intestines need to be long to provide a large internal surface area along which it will take enough time for the contents to pass and be digested and absorbed. If your intestines were short, food would pass through them too quickly and all of the nutrients might not be absorbed. So the intestine coils around on itself to squeeze its entire length into the compact space of your abdomen.

Esophagus

Stomach

The small intestine is about 17 feet (5–6 m) long.

The large intestine is about 5 feet (1.5 m) long.

Rectum

A human body with straight intestines would be nearly 32 feet (10 m) tall!

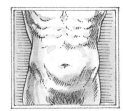

The Stomach

HAVE YOU EVER EATEN a meal so big that you felt you were about to burst? If so, your stomach had probably stretched to hold nearly half a gallon (some two liters) of food. No doubt you complained of a "stomachache" and pointed to your navel area. In fact, the stomach is much higher in the body than most people imagine. It is tucked under the lower left ribs, with its base about level with the lowest rib.

Your stomach is the second stop for food and drink, after your mouth. A J-shaped bag made of several muscle layers, its main job is to break food into smaller pieces for digestion by squeezing it into a sloppy mush. It also breaks down food chemically, by mixing it with acid and digestive chemicals called gastric enzymes, all made in the stomach lining. Few germs can withstand this chemical assault, so the stomach also helps to sterilize the food you eat.

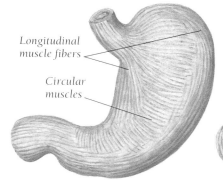

Longitudinal muscle fibers

Circular muscles

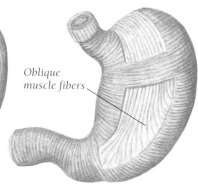

Oblique muscle fibers

OUTER MUSCLE LAYERS

Under its smooth outer coat, the serosa, the stomach has several muscle layers. Two groups of muscle fibers, the longitudinals, run down its sides. Under these are circular muscles, which extend around the entire stomach.

INNER MUSCLE LAYERS

Beneath the circular muscles are diagonal bands of muscle fibers, the obliques. Overall, the three sets of crisscrossing muscles let the stomach contract in almost any direction, to squeeze its contents.

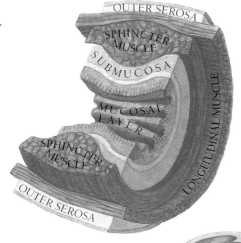

OUTER SEROSA
SPHINCTER MUSCLE
SUBMUCOSA
MUCOSAL LAYER
SPHINCTER MUSCLE
LONGITUDINAL MUSCLE
OUTER SEROSA

PYLORIC SPHINCTER

The gate between the stomach and the small intestine is the pyloric sphincter. It is formed from a ringlike thickening in the circular band of muscle. Usually closed to hold in the stomach contents, it relaxes for a few seconds at a time during digestion. Pressure from the squeezing stomach muscles forces a squirt of chyme into the intestine.

FILLING AND EMPTYING

An average meal takes about six hours to pass through the stomach on its way to the small intestine. Starchy, carbohydrate-rich foods are digested in two or three hours, high-protein foods take slightly longer, and fatty foods may still be trickling from the stomach seven or eight hours after you eat them.

A meal reaches your stomach as a series of soft, saliva-moistened balls, called boluses. With each swallow, food accumulates in your stomach, making it expand like a balloon.

After an hour or two, the food has been mashed and mixed with acid and enzymes to form a creamy liquid called chyme. This is squeezed into the small intestine a little at a time.

Muscular waves in stomach wall

A few hours later, some food oozes through the stomach's exit, the pyloric sphincter, but most is still churning in the stomach. As the stomach empties, it gradually softens and shrinks, like a deflating balloon.

Pyloric sphincter

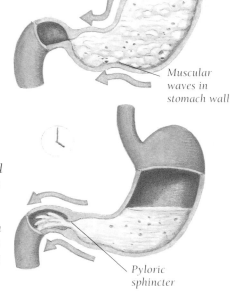

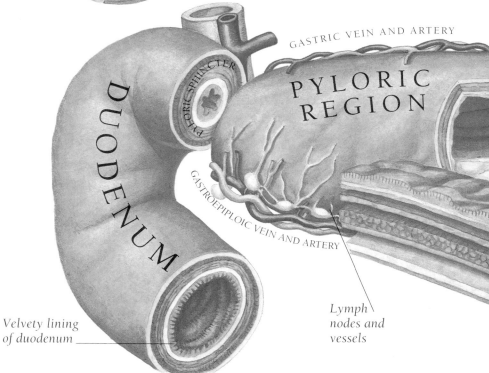

GASTRIC VEIN AND ARTERY

PYLORIC SPHINCTER

DUODENUM

PYLORIC REGION

GASTROEPIPLOIC VEIN AND ARTERY

Velvety lining of duodenum

Lymph nodes and vessels

A big push

The narrow, tubelike section of the stomach nearest to the first part of the small intestine, the duodenum, is known as the pyloric region. When food is ready to leave the stomach and enter the duodenum, the pyloric muscles push out the food in forceful waves called paristaltic contractions.

Arteries and veins

Like all organs, the stomach has its own blood supply. A team of arteries branching from the abdominal aorta brings it fresh, high-oxygen blood. Veins return most of the used, low-oxygen blood back to the heart. But some blood travels instead along branches of the portal vein to the liver. There, substances in the blood absorbed through the stomach wall, such as sugars and alcohols, are processed.

ESOPHAGUS

BOLUS

MUCOSAL LAYER

SUBMUCOSAL LAYER

MUSCLE LAYERS

SEROSAL LAYER

The speed of a swallow

Like the stomach and other parts of the digestive tube, the esophagus has layers of longitudinal and circular muscles in its wall. These muscles contract in waves to squeeze a food bolus down toward the stomach at a rate of about 1.5 inches (4 cm) per second. Gravity helps pull the bolus downward as well, but if you happened to be eating while hanging upside down, your esophagus muscles could do the job alone.

Not a true sphincter

The junction of the esophagus and stomach is sometimes called the cardiac sphincter, because it is near to the heart. Although it cannot open and close as tightly as the pyloric sphincter, the cardiac sphincter is aided by the contraction of other muscles to keep acid and swallowed food from flowing back up the esophagus (a feeling known as "heartburn").

Fundus of stomach

This confusing name for the top of the stomach actually means "bottom." In an operation, the stomach is opened from the patient's front, so the fundus appears to be at the bottom, because the fundus is closest to the paitent's back.

FUNDUS of STOMACH

GASTRIC ARTERY

GASTRIC VEIN

INNER STOMACH

CHYME
SEMIDIGESTED FOOD

MUCOSAL LAYER
INNER STOMACH WALL

OBLIQUE MUSCLE LAYER

CIRCULAR MUSCLE LAYER

LONGITUDINAL MUSCLE LAYER

INNER SEROSAL LAYER

OUTER SEROSAL LAYER

Looking into the stomach

Doctors can peer directly into the stomach using a flexible tube device called a gastroscope. This is a type of endoscope, an instrument for looking into body openings. The gastroscope is carefully threaded down the throat and esophagus, then passed through the cardiac sphincter to reach the stomach. It contains a lighting system to illuminate the interior of the stomach, a fiber-optic system for viewing, and an air line for inflating the stomach, which helps give a good view. The photographs below were taken with the help of a gastroscope.

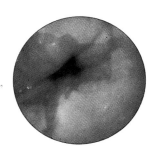

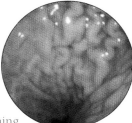

Below is a view of the rugae, the folds lining the stomach.

Above is a view down the esophagus, just before reaching the cardiac sphincter.

Submucosa

This layer of loose, spongy tissue provides a cushion between the mucosa attached to its inner side and the muscle layers on its outer side. The submucosa also contains blood vessels and nerves.

Why you burp

Sometimes when you eat too quickly or drink fizzy drinks, air gets into your stomach along with your food. The air is pushed out of the stomach and up through the esophagus as a burp.

Four-layered wall

Four main layers make up the stomach wall – the red-brown mucosa, the submucosa, the muscularis (or muscle layer), and the serosa. These layers continue throughout most of the digestive tract. The flat, scalelike cells of the inner and outer serosa envelop the entire stomach.

Stomach lining

The velvety texture of the mucosa (inner wall) of the stomach is due to thousands of tiny dents, or pits, contained within it. Specialized groups of cells in the pits make and release hydrochloric acid. Other cells release enzymes such as pepsin, which softens tough meat fibers for easier digestion, and the hormone gastrin, which triggers the production of more gastric juices when food enters and stretches the stomach. As the stomach contracts, its mucosa bunches into folds called rugae.

Barrier of mucus

What keeps the strong meat-digesting chemicals in the stomach from eating away at the stomach itself? The stomach's defense is provided by a coat of slimy mucus. Groups of cells in the lining make a regular supply of mucus to line and protect the interior.

Enough to last a lifetime

An average adult human stomach processes about 1,100 pounds (500 kg) of food each year to keep its body healthy. Over a 70-year lifespan, accounting for smaller meals during childhood, this adds up to more than 33 tons (30,000 kg) of food – equivalent to the weight of six elephants (without tusks!).

The Liver, Pancreas, and Spleen

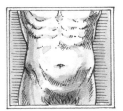

IN TIMES GONE BY, people believed that love and courage came not from the heart, but from the liver. That is why a coward is sometimes called "lily-livered." Of course, it is now known that the brain is the site of emotions and feelings. But the liver is crucial to your well-being. A complex chemical factory with at least 600 different roles in metabolism (body chemistry), it processes and stores body-building nutrients and energy-giving sugars; it filters your blood and recycles its constituents; it detoxifies, making dangerous chemicals harmless; it produces bile for digestion; and it stores vitamins and minerals.

Just to the left of your liver is the pancreas. The pancreas has two distinct roles. One is to manufacture digestive chemicals known as pancreatic enzymes. These pour along a tube into your small intestine, where they help digest food. The other is to make insulin and glucagon, two hormones that control the way your body cells use energy. Also in your upper abdomen is your spleen. It is involved in defense against invading germs and in filtering and maintaining healthy blood.

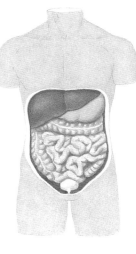

LOCATING THE LIVER
Like the stomach, the liver is higher in the body than many people realize. In fact, its uppermost hump lies just behind your right nipple, under the dome of the diaphragm. The pancreas is on your left side, just behind your stomach. The spleen is tucked behind the left part of your stomach. All these organs are protected by your lower ribs.

INSIDE A LIVER LOBULE
On the outside, the liver looks smooth and slightly rubbery. But it actually consists of about 75,000 tiny lobules. Each lobule, which is about 0.04 inch (1 mm) across and shaped like a hexagon, has a central vein. Sheets of liver cells, or hepatocytes, fan out around it. Spaces between the cells, called sinusoids, are constantly topped up with oxygen-rich blood for the hard-working hepatocytes. Branches of the hepatic artery, portal vein, and hepatic duct surround each lobule.

Hepatic vein

Central vein

Sinusoids

Hepatocytes

Branch of hepatic artery

Branch of hepatic vein

Branch of hepatic duct

Portal vein

Liver lobes
Weighing about 3 pounds (1.4 kg), the liver is the body's largest internal organ. It consists of a large right lobe and a smaller left lobe, divided by the falciform ligament.

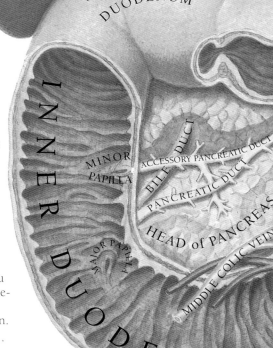

RIGHT LOBE of LIVER

LEFT LOBE

FALCIFORM LIGAMENT

HEPATIC DUCT

GALL BLADDER

BILE DUCT

RIGHT LOBE of LIVER

PERITONEUM

SUPERIOR PART of DUODENUM

INNER DUODENUM

MINOR PAPILLA

ACCESSORY PANCREATIC DUCT

BILE DUCT

PANCREATIC DUCT

MAJOR PAPILLA

HEAD of PANCREAS

MIDDLE COLIC VEIN

Gall bladder
Tucked into a dent under the right lobe of the liver is the gall bladder. This pear-shaped sac is about 4 inches (10 cm) long. It stores bile, a yellowish mixture of fluids, body salts, and wastes assembled by the liver. Bile helps to break up and digest fats in your food.

Double duty
The liver can "cover" for the gall bladder if it is removed, secreting bile directly into the duodenum. In fact, the liver itself is incredibly resilient. You could probably lose about three-quarters of your liver, and it would still continue to function.

Bile tubes
The liver makes about a quart (over a liter) of bile daily. Some trickles directly from the liver into the small intestine, along the hepatic and then the bile ducts. The remainder is stored in the gall bladder. When the stomach squeezes food into the duodenum, a hormone is released to start the gall bladder's muscles squeezing, which squirts bile into the duodenum.

Vitamin store
Vitamins and minerals from the food that you eat – including copper, iron, and vitamins A, D, E, and K – are stored in your liver and released into the bloodstream as needed.

Lymph supply
Lymph fluid oozing from the liver is especially high in protein. Some of this fluid circulates around the vessels and nodes of the lymphatic system. The rest empties back into the blood system by way of one of the main veins near the heart.

A color-enhanced scan of a liver shows the spine (in green) just behind it.

The spleen
The spleen is a spongy, purplish organ found just behind the stomach. Although it is usually slightly smaller than your fist, the spleen can vary greatly in size, depending on your general health and whether you have just eaten. It shares some functions with the rest of the lymphatic system, including making lymphocytes to fight disease.

Blood reserves
Like the liver, the spleen stores extra reserves of blood. In an emergency, nerves signal the spleen to contract and it releases most of its reservoir of blood into circulation.

Red and white pulp
Inside the spleen are patches of white pulp rich in white blood cells and lumps of red pulp where worn-out red blood cells are dismantled and recycled.

Splenic artery
In order to supply the blood-rich spleen, the large splenic artery divides into five branches even before it reaches the organ.

Lymph nodes

Branches of splenic artery and vein

ESOPHAGUS
INNER LIVER
APEX of LIVER
STOMACH
INNER STOMACH
SPLEEN
PERITONEUM
RED PULP
WHITE PULP
GASTRIC ARTERY
GASTRIC VEIN
SPLENIC ARTERY
VENA CAVA
HEPATIC ARTERY
SPLENIC ARTERY
SPLENIC VEIN
PANCREATIC DUCT
TAIL of PANCREAS
PANCREAS
PORTAL VEIN
COLIC ARTERY
COLIC VEIN

The digestive pancreas
Each day, your pancreas makes about a quart (over a liter) of enzyme-packed digestive juices. These flow along tubes called pancreatic ducts to the duodenum, where they help to further digest your last meal. The pancreatic juices also counteract the strong acids in the stomach juices, so that the small intestine is protected from being digested itself.

RECYCLING IN THE SPLEEN
After about 120 days, red blood cells need renewing. The spleen serves as a recycling center for your blood. As blood passes through the spleen, scavenger cells called macrophages (like the ones found in your lungs) take away the worn-out red blood cells. Valuable products such as iron are released and sent back to the blood. The rest of the old cell is broken down and discarded, along with any cells that are misshapen or not working properly.

The hormonal pancreas
Insulin and glucagon, two hormones that regulate the amount of sugar in the blood, are made in microscopic clusters of cells, called islets, embedded in the pancreas. The hormones do not flow along the pancreatic ducts, as the digestive juices do. Instead, they pass from the islets straight into the blood flowing through the pancreas, to be circulated around the whole body.

The renewal process goes on continually, every second.

Portal vein
Unlike any other organ in the body, the liver has two blood supplies. It gets oxygen-rich blood from the hepatic artery, a branch of the aorta. But an additional supply of blood, rich in nutrients, comes from the stomach and intestines, through the portal vein.

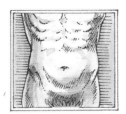

The Intestines

EACH MOUTHFUL OF FOOD is gnashed by your teeth for a minute or so, squeezed down your esophagus in about 10 seconds, and pulped in your stomach for two to four hours. After this, it is ready to enter your small and large intestines, where almost everything your body can use is extracted and absorbed.

Coiled intricately into your abdomen, the intestines form the largest portion of your digestive tract's length. Your small intestine is narrow, but long. It takes between one and six hours for food to travel through its 16- to 19-foot (5- to 6-m) length. The small intestine continues the chemical digestion of food that started in your mouth and stomach by bombarding its soupy contents with more enzymes and digestive juices. Most of the resulting nutrients are absorbed into the blood and lymph vessels within its walls. At about 5 feet (1.5 m) long, your large intestine is shorter than the small intestine, but it is much wider. Its main roles are to absorb water and useful minerals from your food and to prepare the leftovers for expulsion through the muscular ring that forms the final part of the tract, the anus.

Mesentery
The mesentery is part of the peritoneum, the thin membrane lining the inside wall of the abdomen. From its narrow end anchored to the rear abdominal wall, the mesentery fans out to wrap around the coils of the intestine. It carries blood and lymph to and from the intestine and holds it in place so that it does not twist itself into knots.

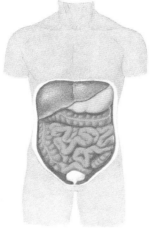

INSIDE THE DIGESTIVE TUBES
In the drawing of the small and large intestines on the right, the stomach and liver have been lifted away. The small intestine and the fatty pad known as the greater omentum are pulled to the left, stretching out the mesentery behind them. This reveals the loop of the large intestine, enriched with a web of mesenteric blood vessels.

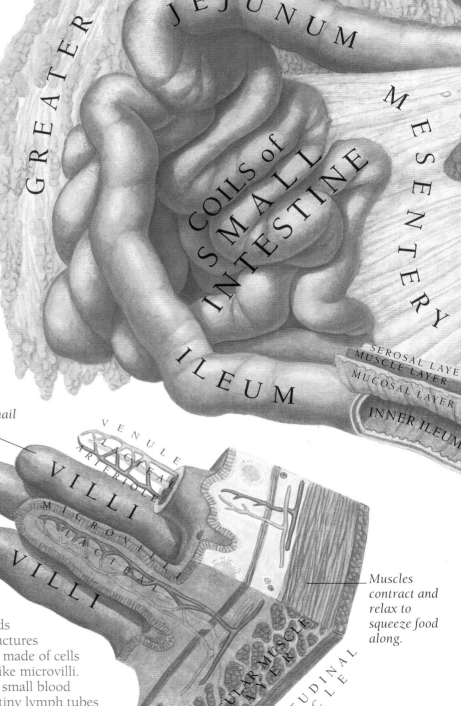

GREATER OMENTUM

JEJUNUM

MESENTERY

COILS of SMALL INTESTINE

ILEUM

SEROSAL LAYER
MUSCLE LAYER
MUCOSAL LAYER

INNER ILEUM

THE BODY'S GUTS
The small intestine folds and twists inside the center of the abdomen, below the stomach, liver, and pancreas. The large intestine runs up the right side of the abdomen, across under the liver and stomach, and down the left side. It forms a "picture frame" around the small intestine, called the colonic loop.

An area of the intestinal wall about the size of your fingernail contains about 3,000 villi.

Each villus is about 0.04 inch (1 mm) long.

VENULE
LACTEAL
ARTERIOLE
VILLI
MICROVILLI
LACTEAL
VILLI

Muscles contract and relax to squeeze food along.

FINGERS FOR FOOD
The inner lining of your small intestine is not smooth like a garden hose, but folded and ridged, with a velvety texture. Within these folds are thousands of tiny finger-shaped structures called villi. The outside of each villus is made of cells that are covered with hundreds of hairlike microvilli. Inside each villus is a dense network of small blood vessels, the arterioles and venules, and tiny lymph tubes known as lacteals. Nutrients from the food passing through the intestine seep through the thin covering of the microvilli into the blood and lymph tubes of the villi. There, they are carried away to nourish your body tissues. Together, the folds, ridges, villi, and microvilli increase the surface area of the small intestine by eight times, making digestion faster and more efficient.

CIRCULAR MUSCLE LAYER
LONGITUDINAL MUSCLE

Mucosal layer contains venules, arterioles, and thin muscle sheets.

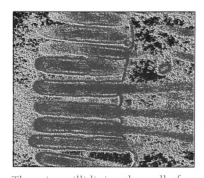

The microvilli lining the wall of the duodenum are shown in red in this color-enhanced micrograph, magnified about 20,000 times.

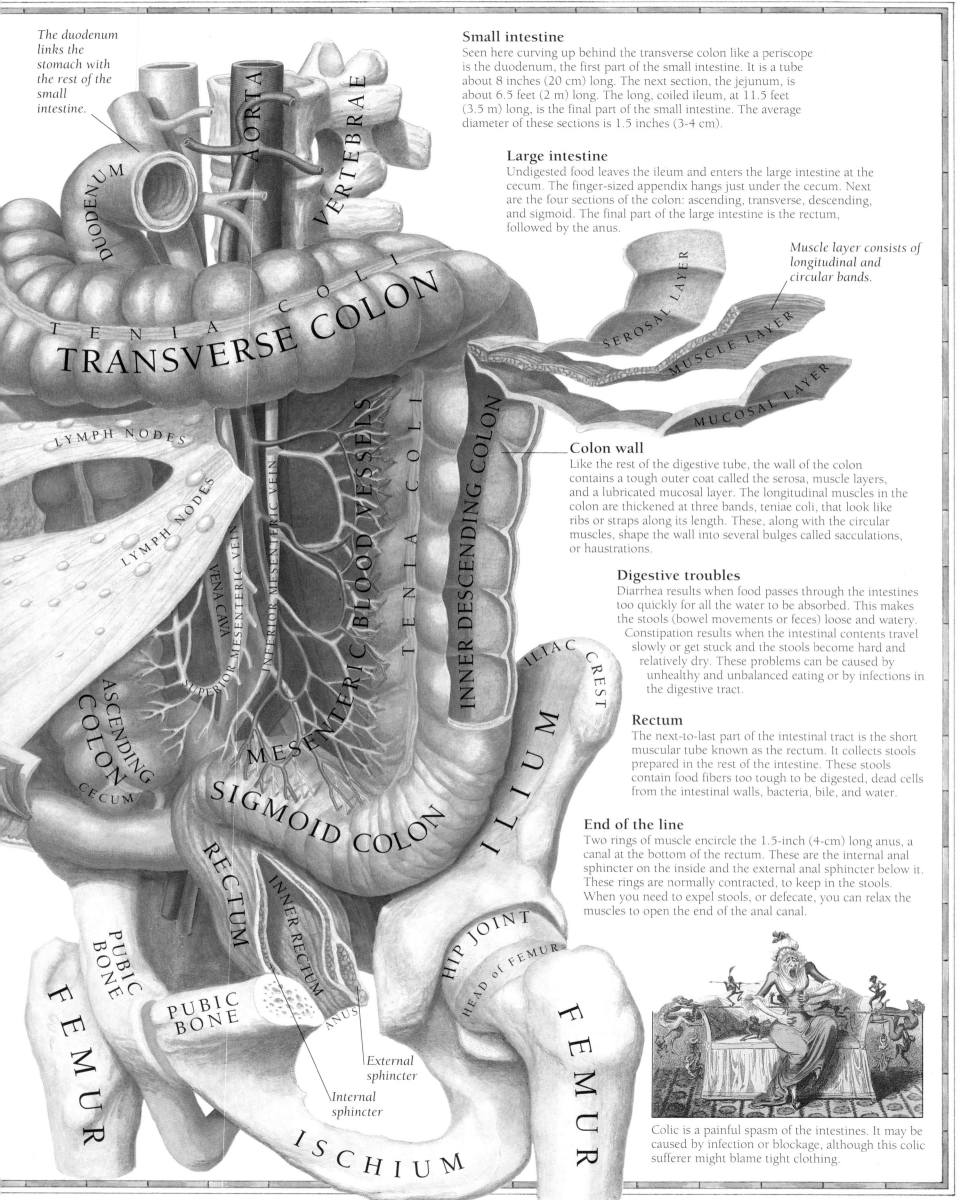

The duodenum links the stomach with the rest of the small intestine.

DUODENUM

AORTA

VERTEBRAE

TENIA COLI

TRANSVERSE COLON

LYMPH NODES

LYMPH NODES

VENA CAVA

SUPERIOR MESENTERIC VEIN

INFERIOR MESENTERIC VEIN

MESENTERIC BLOOD VESSELS

TENIA COLI

INNER DESCENDING COLON

SEROSAL LAYER

MUSCLE LAYER

MUCOSAL LAYER

ASCENDING COLON

CECUM

MESENTERIC

SIGMOID COLON

ILIAC CREST

ILIUM

RECTUM

INNER RECTUM

PUBIC BONE

PUBIC BONE

ANUS

HIP JOINT

HEAD of FEMUR

FEMUR

FEMUR

ISCHIUM

External sphincter

Internal sphincter

Small intestine

Seen here curving up behind the transverse colon like a periscope is the duodenum, the first part of the small intestine. It is a tube about 8 inches (20 cm) long. The next section, the jejunum, is about 6.5 feet (2 m) long. The long, coiled ileum, at 11.5 feet (3.5 m) long, is the final part of the small intestine. The average diameter of these sections is 1.5 inches (3-4 cm).

Large intestine

Undigested food leaves the ileum and enters the large intestine at the cecum. The finger-sized appendix hangs just under the cecum. Next are the four sections of the colon: ascending, transverse, descending, and sigmoid. The final part of the large intestine is the rectum, followed by the anus.

Muscle layer consists of longitudinal and circular bands.

Colon wall

Like the rest of the digestive tube, the wall of the colon contains a tough outer coat called the serosa, muscle layers, and a lubricated mucosal layer. The longitudinal muscles in the colon are thickened at three bands, teniae coli, that look like ribs or straps along its length. These, along with the circular muscles, shape the wall into several bulges called sacculations, or haustrations.

Digestive troubles

Diarrhea results when food passes through the intestines too quickly for all the water to be absorbed. This makes the stools (bowel movements or feces) loose and watery. Constipation results when the intestinal contents travel slowly or get stuck and the stools become hard and relatively dry. These problems can be caused by unhealthy and unbalanced eating or by infections in the digestive tract.

Rectum

The next-to-last part of the intestinal tract is the short muscular tube known as the rectum. It collects stools prepared in the rest of the intestine. These stools contain food fibers too tough to be digested, dead cells from the intestinal walls, bacteria, bile, and water.

End of the line

Two rings of muscle encircle the 1.5-inch (4-cm) long anus, a canal at the bottom of the rectum. These are the internal anal sphincter on the inside and the external anal sphincter below it. These rings are normally contracted, to keep in the stools. When you need to expel stools, or defecate, you can relax the muscles to open the end of the anal canal.

Colic is a painful spasm of the intestines. It may be caused by infection or blockage, although this colic sufferer might blame tight clothing.

The Kidneys and Bladder

LEFTOVERS FROM DIGESTION are dealt with by your intestines. But dozens of waste products from chemical reactions build up inside your cells. These wastes seep into your blood, which carries them around your body to a pair of complex organs especially designed to filter the blood as it passes through – the kidneys. They extract the wastes, along with unwanted minerals and excess water, and prepare it for removal. The fluid waste is called urine. Day and night, urine trickles from the kidneys along two tubes known as ureters, to your bladder, a stretchable storage bag near the base of your abdomen. By the time it expands to the size of your clenched fist, sensors in its walls are telling your brain that it's time to get rid of the urine. You relax the urethral sphincter, a ring of muscle, around the exit of your bladder. Muscles in the bladder wall squeeze the urine along a tube called the urethra and out of your body.

POSITION IN THE BODY
The two kidneys are higher in the body than many people realize. They are tucked into the rear upper abdomen, not far below the tips of the lungs, behind the lower parts of the liver and stomach, and shielded by the lowest ribs. They are not quite mirror images: The right kidney is usually 0.4–0.8 inch (1–2 cm) lower than the left one.

Lung
Liver
Stomach
Kidney
Bladder

INSIDE THE KIDNEY
About one million tiny filters, called nephrons, cleanse blood. As the blood flows through a nephron's microscopic knot of capillaries, the glomerulus, wastes and water are forced into a cup-shaped capsule around it. Then they flow along a U-shaped tubule, where much of the water and useful minerals soak back into the blood. The remains trickle into the system of urine-collecting tubes.

Your kidneys also help balance the amount of water in your body. The water you lose daily as sweat, urine, or vapor in your breath, needs to be replaced. If you do not obtain enough water from your meals and drinks, your kidneys reduce the amount of urine they produce. If you get a great deal of water, they speed up production.

Emergency glands
One suprarenal, or adrenal, gland sits at the top of each kidney. These glands make hormones that help you act quickly when faced with an emergency.

The kidney areas are named after the organs over them.

Medulla
The inner kidney, or medulla, contains about 15 fanlike groups of collecting tubes for urine. These are separated by renal columns containing blood vessels.

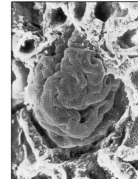
A computer-colored micrograph of a nephron shows the knotlike glomerulus (in orange), with the capsule (gold) around it.

Down the tubes
Urine passes through tiny holes at the bottom of the medulla called papillae, into a minor calyx. These tubes join to form larger ones, the major calyces, which eventually drain into an even bigger cavity called the renal pelvis.

Ureter
Each ureter is about 1 foot (30 cm) long. For most of its length, it is as thick as the inner ink-holding tube of a ballpoint pen. But it is not a motionless, hollow tube that urine rushes through, like water in a garden hose. Instead, the muscles in its thick walls contract in waves to push urine downward, into the bladder in a series of small spurts.

Renal blood vessels
Renal means having to do with the kidneys. The wide, short renal arteries, one to each kidney, bring plenty of blood – about a third of a gallon (over 1.2 liters) each minute – to each kidney. This means that all the blood in your body passes through each kidney 400 times in one day. More than 99.9% of this volume leaves the kidney along the renal vein. Less than 0.1% is filtered out as urine.

KIDNEY

COLIC AREA
SPLENIC AREA
GASTRIC AREA
SUPRARENAL AREA
PANCREATIC AREA
JEJUNAL AREA

CORTEX of KIDNEY
MEDULLA
MINOR CALYX
MAJOR CALYX
PAPILLA
RENAL COLUMN
MEDULLA
CORTEX
RENAL CAPSULE
FAT
PELVIS of KIDNEY

BRANCH of ARTERY
BRANCH of VEIN

SUPRARENAL GLAND
MEDULLA of GLAND
CAPSULE of GLAND
INFERIOR PHRENIC VEIN

RENAL ARTERY
RENAL VEIN
TESTICULAR ARTERY
TESTICULAR VEIN

URETER

Urine-collecting tube

Small vein
Small artery
U-shaped tubule in renal medulla
Capillary network absorbs water and minerals
Glomerulus and capsule in renal cortex
Each kidney is wrapped in a layer of tissue called the renal capsule.

MEDULLA
RENAL CORTEX
RENAL CAPSULE

48

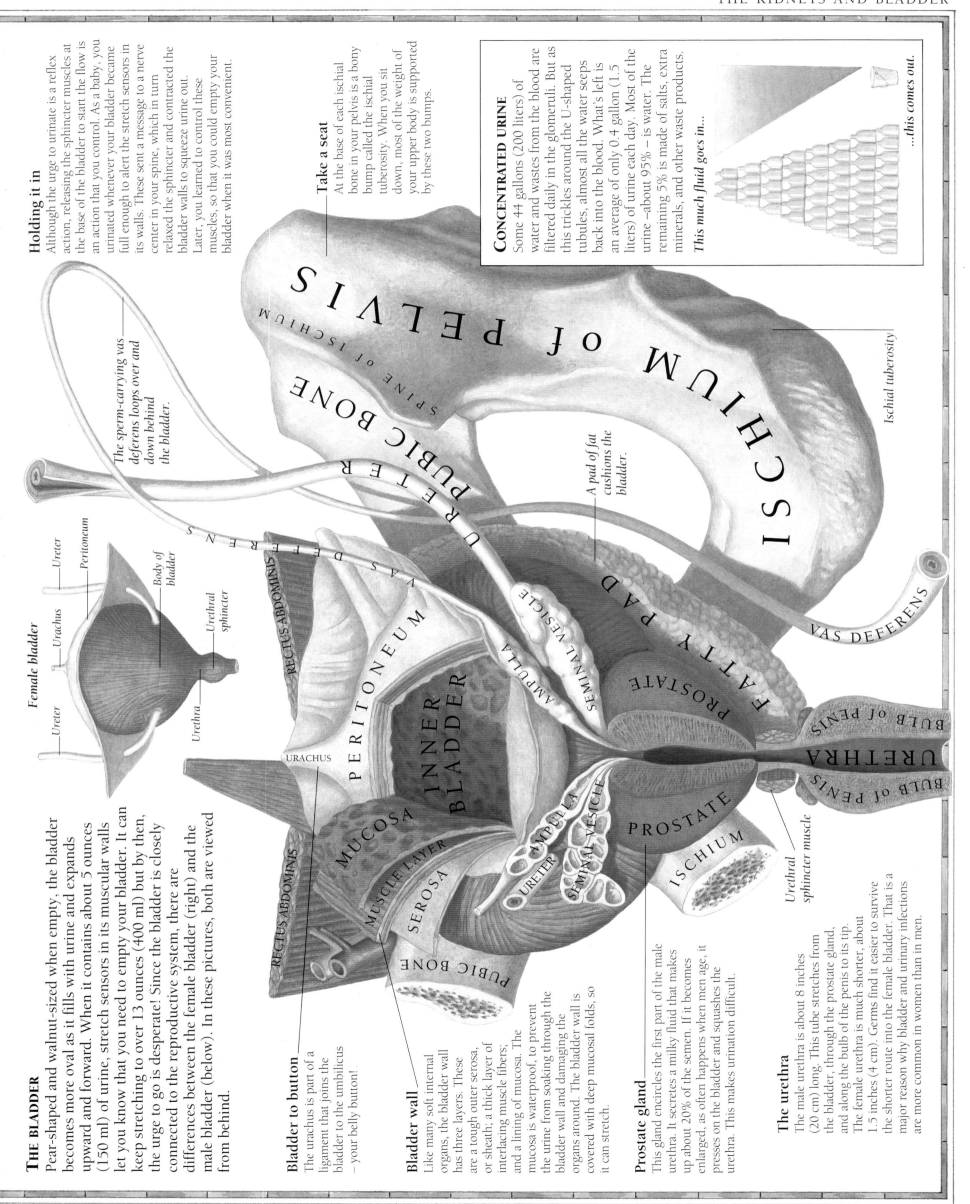

THE BLADDER

Pear-shaped and walnut-sized when empty, the bladder becomes more oval as it fills with urine and expands upward and forward. When it contains about 5 ounces (150 ml) of urine, stretch sensors in its muscular walls let you know that you need to empty your bladder. It can keep stretching to over 13 ounces (400 ml) but by then, the urge to go is desperate! Since the bladder is closely connected to the reproductive system, there are differences between the female bladder (right) and the male bladder (below). In these pictures, both are viewed from behind.

Bladder to button
The urachus is part of a ligament that joins the bladder to the umbilicus – your belly button!

Bladder wall
Like many soft internal organs, the bladder wall has three layers. These are a tough outer serosa, or sheath; a thick layer of interlacing muscle fibers; and a lining of mucosa. The mucosa is waterproof, to prevent the urine from soaking through the bladder wall and damaging the organs around. The bladder wall is covered with deep mucosal folds, so it can stretch.

Prostate gland
This gland encircles the first part of the male urethra. It secretes a milky fluid that makes up about 20% of the semen. If it becomes enlarged, as often happens when men age, it presses on the bladder and squashes the urethra. This makes urination difficult.

The urethra
The male urethra is about 8 inches (20 cm) long. This tube stretches from the bladder, through the prostate gland, and along the bulb of the penis to its tip. The female urethra is much shorter, about 1.5 inches (4 cm). Germs find it easier to survive the shorter route into the female bladder. That is a major reason why bladder and urinary infections are more common in women than in men.

Holding it in
Although the urge to urinate is a reflex action, releasing the sphincter muscles at the base of the bladder to start the flow is an action that you control. As a baby, you urinated whenever your bladder became full enough to alert the stretch sensors in its walls. These sent a message to a nerve center in your spine, which in turn relaxed the sphincter and contracted the bladder walls to squeeze urine out. Later, you learned to control these muscles, so that you could empty your bladder when it was most convenient.

Take a seat
At the base of each ischial bone in your pelvis is a bony bump called the ischial tuberosity. When you sit down, most of the weight of your upper body is supported by these two bumps.

CONCENTRATED URINE
Some 44 gallons (200 liters) of water and wastes from the blood are filtered daily in the glomeruli. But as this trickles around the U-shaped tubules, almost all the water seeps back into the blood. What's left is an average of only 0.4 gallon (1.5 liters) of urine each day. Most of the urine –about 95% – is water. The remaining 5% is made of salts, extra minerals, and other waste products.
This much fluid goes in...

...this comes out.

Labels on illustration:
- *Female bladder*
- Ureter
- Urachus
- Peritoneum
- *Body of bladder*
- Ureter
- *Urethral sphincter*
- Urethra
- *The sperm-carrying vas deferens loops over and down behind the bladder.*
- ISCHIUM of PELVIS
- SPINE of ISCHIUM
- PUBIC BONE
- URETER
- VAS DEFERENS
- RECTUS ABDOMINIS
- PERITONEUM
- URACHUS
- INNER BLADDER
- MUCOSA
- MUSCLE LAYER
- SEROSA
- PUBIC BONE
- RECTUS ABDOMINIS
- AMPULLA
- SEMINAL VESICLE
- A pad of fat cushions the bladder.
- FATTY PAD
- PROSTATE
- BULB of PENIS
- URETHRA
- BULB of PENIS
- PROSTATE
- SEMINAL VESICLE
- AMPULLA
- URETER
- ISCHIUM
- *Urethral sphincter muscle*
- Ischial tuberosity

49

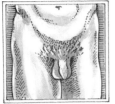

The Lower Torso – Male

THE MOST OBVIOUS DIFFERENCES between the male and the female body are in the reproductive organs of the lower abdomen. The male sex organs are specialized to produce and deliver sperm, the microscopic tadpole-shaped cells needed to fertilize the eggs of a female. Sperm production begins at puberty, when a boy becomes sexually mature, and continues into old age. The sperm are produced inside the testes. During sexual intercourse, they travel along a tube called the vas deferens to the penis, where they leave the man's body and enter the woman's. This is a reflex action called ejaculation.

The reproductive organs, also known as the sexual or genital organs, are closely connected with the parts of the excretory (urinary) system. In men, the urethra is the tube used for both the passage of sperm-containing semen (seminal fluid) and the flow of urine during urination.

SYMBOL OF FERTILITY
Many cultures focus on the reproductive organs as symbols of fertility and fruitfulness, strength, and power. Examples include an enlarged penis in a man, and the exaggerated contours of the breasts and hips in a woman. Some societies disapprove of, and even ban, these age-old images.

The "Cerne Giant," brandishing his club, is carved into the chalky North Dorset Downs in southern England.

THE PATH OF SPERM
During sexual arousal and ejaculation, the sperm follow a tortuous pathway (shown in blue below) from their site of development in the testes, through the penis, and out of the man's body. Along the way, several glandular organs contribute to the seminal fluid. These include two seminal vesicles behind the bladder, the prostate around the urethra, and two Cowper's, or bulbourethral, glands at the base of the penis. The fluid provides nutrients and chemicals to help the sperm on their way.

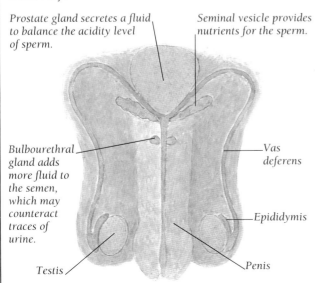

Prostate gland secretes a fluid to balance the acidity level of sperm.

Seminal vesicle provides nutrients for the sperm.

Bulbourethral gland adds more fluid to the semen, which may counteract traces of urine.

Vas deferens

Epididymis

Penis

Testis

INSIDE AND OUT
The male reproductive organs are partly inside the lower abdomen and partly hanging below it. Inside are glands, such as the walnut-sized prostate, and tubes, such as the vas deferens, that link the organs. Outside are the penis and the bag of skin called the scrotum, which hangs behind it. Suspended in the scrotum are the pair of egg-shaped testes, in which sperm cells are manufactured.

Vas deferens
The vas deferens is a 16-inch (40-cm) tube that carries sperm from each testis and epididymis (a long coiled tube at the base of the vas deferens where sperm mature) to the penis. The vas deferens curls up and around the back of the bladder and down under it, toward the urethra. Just behind the base of the prostate, it joins the tube from the seminal vesicle and forms the ejaculatory duct, which then joins the main urethra.

Penis
The penis transfers the sperm to the woman's body during sexual intercourse. The main part of the penis consists of three spongy cylinders: two corpora cavernosa (one of which can be seen above) and the corpus spongiosum. During sexual arousal, these fill up with blood, making the penis erect – that is, longer, thicker, and stiffer.

The loose flap of skin over the glans is called the foreskin.

ILIAC CREST of PELVIS

SKIN

ILIACUS MUSCLE

TRANSVERSE ABDOMINAL

INTERNAL ABDOMINAL OBLIQUE

EXTERNAL ABDOMINAL OBLIQUE

LATERAL CUTANEOUS NERVE of THIGH

FEMORAL NERVE

URETER

TESTICULAR VEIN AND ARTERY

VAS DEFERENS

FATTY LAYER

PUBIC BONE

SUSPENSORY LIGAMENT

RIGHT LEG

SKIN

FATTY LAYER

DORSAL ARTERY AND VEIN of PENIS

CORPUS CAVERNOSUM

PENIS

CORPUS SPONGIOSUM

SKIN

FORESKIN

GLANS PENIS

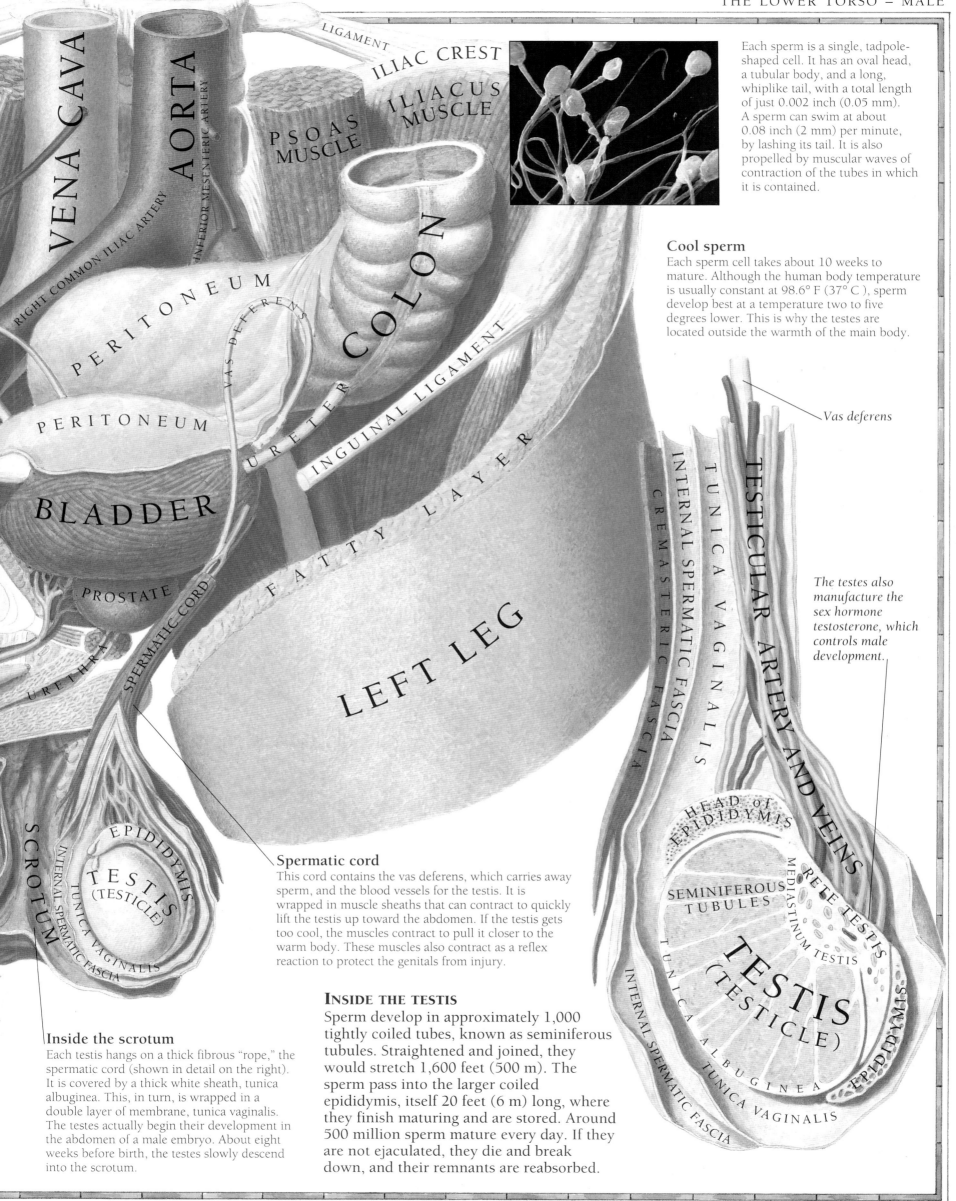

VENA CAVA

AORTA

RIGHT COMMON ILIAC ARTERY

INFERIOR MESENTERIC ARTERY

LIGAMENT

ILIAC CREST

PSOAS MUSCLE

ILIACUS MUSCLE

PERITONEUM

COLON

VAS DEFERENS

PERITONEUM

URETER

INGUINAL LIGAMENT

BLADDER

FATTY LAYER

LEFT LEG

SPERMATIC CORD

PROSTATE

URETHRA

EPIDIDYMIS

INTERNAL SPERMATIC FASCIA

SCROTUM

TESTIS (TESTICLE)

TUNICA VAGINALIS

INTERNAL SPERMATIC FASCIA

CREMASTERIC FASCIA

INTERNAL SPERMATIC FASCIA

TUNICA VAGINALIS

TESTICULAR ARTERY AND VEINS

HEAD of EPIDIDYMIS

SEMINIFEROUS TUBULES

MEDIASTINUM TESTIS

RETE TESTIS

TESTIS (TESTICLE)

TUNICA ALBUGINEA

TUNICA VAGINALIS

EPIDIDYMIS

Each sperm is a single, tadpole-shaped cell. It has an oval head, a tubular body, and a long, whiplike tail, with a total length of just 0.002 inch (0.05 mm). A sperm can swim at about 0.08 inch (2 mm) per minute, by lashing its tail. It is also propelled by muscular waves of contraction of the tubes in which it is contained.

Cool sperm
Each sperm cell takes about 10 weeks to mature. Although the human body temperature is usually constant at 98.6° F (37° C), sperm develop best at a temperature two to five degrees lower. This is why the testes are located outside the warmth of the main body.

Vas deferens

The testes also manufacture the sex hormone testosterone, which controls male development.

Spermatic cord
This cord contains the vas deferens, which carries away sperm, and the blood vessels for the testis. It is wrapped in muscle sheaths that can contract to quickly lift the testis up toward the abdomen. If the testis gets too cool, the muscles contract to pull it closer to the warm body. These muscles also contract as a reflex reaction to protect the genitals from injury.

INSIDE THE TESTIS
Sperm develop in approximately 1,000 tightly coiled tubes, known as seminiferous tubules. Straightened and joined, they would stretch 1,600 feet (500 m). The sperm pass into the larger coiled epididymis, itself 20 feet (6 m) long, where they finish maturing and are stored. Around 500 million sperm mature every day. If they are not ejaculated, they die and break down, and their remnants are reabsorbed.

Inside the scrotum
Each testis hangs on a thick fibrous "rope," the spermatic cord (shown in detail on the right). It is covered by a thick white sheath, tunica albuginea. This, in turn, is wrapped in a double layer of membrane, tunica vaginalis. The testes actually begin their development in the abdomen of a male embryo. About eight weeks before birth, the testes slowly descend into the scrotum.

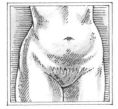

The Lower Torso – Female

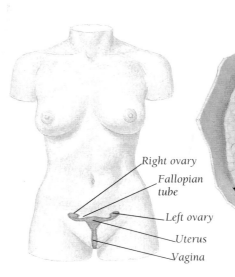

ALTHOUGH THE FEMALE and male reproductive organs look quite different on the outside, there are important parallels within. Men possess sperm-making testes and women have egg-making ovaries. Sperm travel along the vas deferens, whereas eggs travel along the fallopian tubes (oviducts). But one organ is unique to women, enabling them to protect and nurture a fertilized egg as it grows and develops into a baby: the pear-shaped, muscular-walled uterus, or womb.

Every four weeks or so, depending on the timing of the menstrual cycle (explained opposite), an egg, or ovum, ripens in one of the two ovaries. The egg bursts from the ovary and is caught by the wispy "fingers" at the trumpet-shaped end of the fallopian tube. It is carried along the tube by a combination of massaging by the muscles in the tube wall and waving movements of the tiny hairlike cilia in its lining. If sperm are present in the fallopian tube, this is the most common place for fertilization. The egg continues its journey and emerges into the womb. If it is not fertilized, it disintegrates and is expelled during menstruation.

Right ovary
Fallopian tube
Left ovary
Uterus
Vagina

THE REPRODUCTIVE ORGANS
The main organs of the female reproductive system – the uterus, ovaries, and vagina – are inside the body rather than outside it, as in the male system. The uterus is about 3 inches (7 cm) long and 2 inches (5 cm) wide, unless it contains a baby!

SKIN
ILIAC CREST OF PELVIS
ILIACUS MUSCLE
TRANSVERSE ABDOMINAL MUSCLE
INTERNAL ABDOMINAL OBLIQUE
EXTERNAL ABDOMINAL OBLIQUE
FATTY LAYER

INSIDE THE FEMALE ABDOMEN
The reproductive organs nestle deep in the abdomen, beneath the intestines, in front of the lumbar (lower) vertebrae, and just behind the bladder. All of these organs are protected by the deep bowl formed by the bones of the surrounding pelvis, from the iliacs at the sides to the pelvic bones at the front.

SUSPENSORY OVARIAN LIGAMENT

Each ovary is firmly anchored to the uterus and the abdominal wall by ovarian ligaments, tough folds of membrane that wrap around blood vessels and nerves.

AMPULLA of FALLOPIAN TUBE
OVARY
FALLOPIAN TUBE

The uterine ligament is one of several that secure the uterus to the sides of the lower abdomen.

UTERINE LIGAMENT
WALL of UTERUS
FUNDUS of UTERUS
BODY of UTERUS
OVARY
FALLOPIAN TUBE
CERVIX
CERVIX
VAGINAL OS

Bulges in the surface of the ovary show where the eggs are ripening within.

VAGINA
MUCOSAL LAYER
MUSCULARIS LAYER
VAGINAL WALL

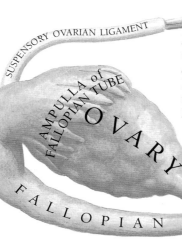

OVARIES AND UTERUS
The uterus is shaped like an upside-down pear, with a wide upper part, called the body, narrowing to the cervix. The opening of the cervix is called the os, which means "mouth" in Latin. The fallopian tubes, each about 4 inches (10 cm) long, curve from the uterus to the ovaries. Each ovary is about the size of a large almond. Inside them, tiny eggs smaller than the dot on this "i" mature in sacs called follicles. A lifetime's supply of immature eggs – about 600,000 – is present at birth, but only around 400 mature during a woman's life. The ovaries also make the female hormones estrogen and progesterone.

This color-enhanced scanning electron micrograph shows a ripe egg (in red) bursting from its follicle inside an ovary.

Folds in the inner mucosal layer of the vagina, called rugae, straighten out during intercourse or childbirth, as the vagina expands.

Under the mucosal layer is a layer of strong interwoven muscle fibers.

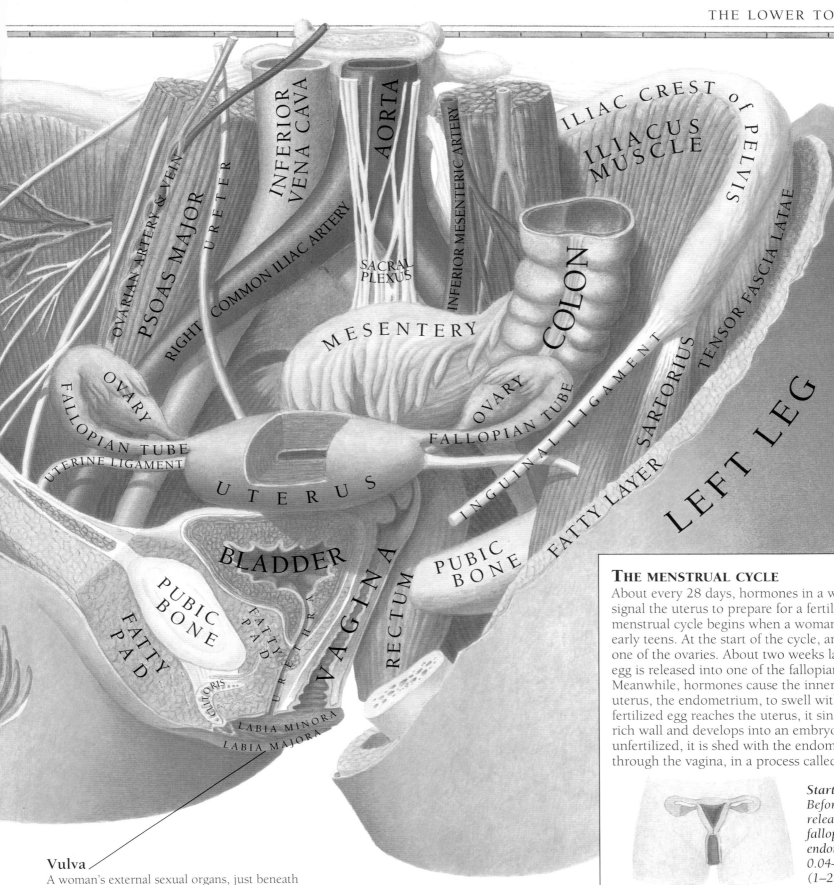

ILIAC CREST of PELVIS

ILIACUS MUSCLE

OVARIAN ARTERY & VEIN

PSOAS MAJOR

URETER

INFERIOR VENA CAVA

AORTA

INFERIOR MESENTERIC ARTERY

RIGHT COMMON ILIAC ARTERY

SACRAL PLEXUS

MESENTERY

COLON

TENSOR FASCIA LATAE

OVARY

FALLOPIAN TUBE

UTERINE LIGAMENT

OVARY

FALLOPIAN TUBE

INGUINAL LIGAMENT

SARTORIUS

LEFT LEG

UTERUS

BLADDER

VAGINA

RECTUM

PUBIC BONE

FATTY LAYER

PUBIC BONE

FATTY PAD

FATTY PAD

URETHRA

CLITORIS

LABIA MINORA

LABIA MAJORA

Vulva
A woman's external sexual organs, just beneath
the fatty pad covering the pubic bone, are known
together as the vulva. Folds of skin called the labia
majora enclose smaller folds, the labia minora,
which protect the entrances to the vagina and
urethra. These folds also shield the clitoris, a tiny
organ richly supplied with blood vessels and
nerves. Like the male penis, it swells with blood
and becomes sensitive during sexual arousal.

Division of roles
Unlike the male urethra, which is a dual-
purpose tube for both urine and sperm,
the female urethra carries only urine. This
tube stretches about 1.5 inches (4 cm)
from the exit of the bladder to an opening
on the vulva – about one-fifth the length of
the male urethra.

HOW SPERM AND EGG JOIN
Sperm enter the female reproductive system during sexual
intercourse. The vagina stretches and its walls secrete fluid
to ease the entry of the erect male penis. At the man's climax
of intercourse, he ejaculates, or releases sperm-carrying
seminal fluid. This flows into the upper end of the vagina,
seeps through the cervix into the space inside the uterus, and
up the narrow tunnels of the fallopian tubes, carrying
sperm to meet any egg that is present.

THE MENSTRUAL CYCLE
About every 28 days, hormones in a woman's body
signal the uterus to prepare for a fertilized egg. This
menstrual cycle begins when a woman reaches her
early teens. At the start of the cycle, an egg ripens in
one of the ovaries. About two weeks later, the ripe
egg is released into one of the fallopian tubes.
Meanwhile, hormones cause the inner lining of the
uterus, the endometrium, to swell with blood. If a
fertilized egg reaches the uterus, it sinks into this
rich wall and develops into an embryo. If the egg is
unfertilized, it is shed with the endometrium
through the vagina, in a process called menstruation.

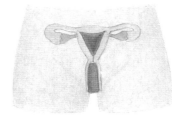

Start of cycle
*Before the egg is
released into the
fallopian tube, the
endometrium is about
0.04–0.06 inches
(1–2 mm) thick.*

Middle of cycle
*The hormone
progesterone causes the
endometrium to swell
with blood and other
fluids, thickening to
about 0.2–0.3 inches
(5–8 mm).*

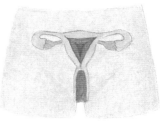

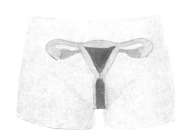

End of cycle
*If the egg is not
fertilized, the
endometrium breaks
down and seeps from
the vagina over the
course of 5–7 days as
menstrual blood flow.*

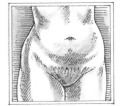

The Development of a Baby

A BABY STARTS TO DEVELOP when just one sperm cell from the father joins and fertilizes an egg cell from the mother. The resulting single cell immediately begins a wondrous series of cell divisions that, over hours and days, will gradually shape a tiny human body. About a week after fertilization, the growing cluster of cells embeds itself in the lining of the uterus. During the next six or seven days, the hollow ball of cells divides into two main parts. The embryo develops in one section. After time, it will receive nourishment from the mother's blood via the other section, which develops into the placenta and umbilical cord.

In general, the baby's development is "head first." The spinal column and brain appear very early, then the other parts of the head, the heart, and vital organs in the torso, followed by the arms and legs. About two months after fertilization, the baby is as big as your thumb – yet it has all of its main body parts.

The period when the baby grows in the mother's uterus is called pregnancy. On average, it lasts 38 weeks from conception and ends on the baby's birthday.

Fertilization

This photomicrograph shows the head of a sperm cell, the pink "ball" lower right, about to merge into the relatively huge egg cell. Several hours later, the fertilized egg divides into two cells. These divide, in turn, and so on. After five days, the cells form a hollow ball called a blastocyst, which floats free in the uterus.

Implantation

About 7-10 days after fertilization, the outside layer of the pinpoint-sized blastocyst has broken down and it has begun to "burrow" its way into the wall of the uterus. This stage is called implantation. The uterine lining is richly supplied with blood vessels, so the blastocyst is surrounded by nourishment. Arched layers of cells inside the ball will become the baby.

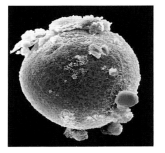

Wall of uterus

These cells form the placenta.

These cells form the embryo.

Embryonic growth

Cells continue to multiply and move, and begin to develop into different types and shapes, such as nerve cells and blood cells. About three weeks after fertilization, two large bulges mark the growing brain. In the eight weeks after fertilization, the developing baby is called an embryo.

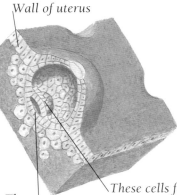

Brain

Spinal cord

Wall of uterus

Yolk sac provides nutrients.

From embryo to fetus

Two months after fertilization, huge changes have taken place. The baby is recognizably human, with a face, eyes, ears, mouth, and all of its major organs. Although the baby looks fully formed, it isn't. It couldn't survive outside its mother at this point. It floats in its own private "swimming pool" of amniotic fluid, warm and cushioned from knocks and jolts. From this time until birth, it is called a fetus.

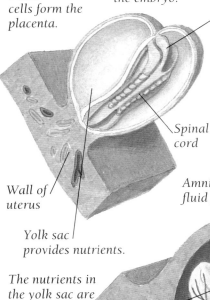

Amniotic fluid

The nutrients in the yolk sac are almost used up. It will shrink and wither away.

Developing placenta

The body stalk connects to the remains of the yolk sac. It is now the umbilical cord.

Between the eighth week of pregnancy and birth, the length of the fetus will increase more than 20 times.

THE PLACENTA

This organ is about the size and shape of a dinner plate – which is apt, since it passes food from mother to baby. Used blood (shown here in blue), low in oxygen and nutrients, flows from the baby's heart along two umbilical arteries to the placenta. There it absorbs oxygen and nutrients and gets rid of wastes. Refreshed and "red" again, the blood flows back to the baby along the umbilical vein.

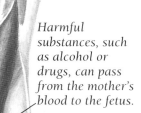

AMNION

PLACENTA

BLOOD VESSEL NETWORK

MATERNAL SURFACE

UMBILICAL CORD

AMNION

UMBILICAL ARTERY

UMBILICAL ARTERY

UMBILICAL VEIN

Pool of mother's blood

The placenta makes hormones that help control pregnancy and birth.

Harmful substances, such as alcohol or drugs, can pass from the mother's blood to the fetus.

The fetus's blood passes through tiny vessels that run through pools of the mother's blood. The blood supplies do not actually mix.

The umbilical cord is about 20 inches (50 cm) long and 0.4-0.8 inches (1-2 cm) thick. The blood vessels are embedded in a tough, gellike substance that prevents kinks and tight knots from forming.

WAITING FOR BIRTH

Nine months after fertilization, this fully developed fetus is waiting to be born. It still has the lifeline of the umbilical cord and receives oxygen and nutrients from the placenta. Within seconds of birth, its hearty cries will open up its own lungs and drain the amniotic fluid from them, so that it can take its first breaths of air.

Expanding uterus squeezes organs above.

The site of the placenta varies. In this pregnancy, it has formed at the front of the uterus.

Myometrium (muscle layer) of uterus

Changes in the uterus

The muscular wall of the uterus stretches enormously as the fetus grows. It is now the largest muscle in the mother's body. It contracts strongly and periodically at birth, to push the baby through the cervix and vagina, out into the world.

Fetal membranes and fluid

The fetus is wrapped in two thin, semitransparent "bags," or membranes. The inner one is called the amnion and contains about 1 litre (1.76 pints) of amniotic fluid, which the fetus swallows and into which it urinates. The fluid contains small quantities of proteins, fats, sugars, minerals, hormones, and enzymes. The outer membrane, the chorion, comes from the same cells that formed the placenta.

By the seventh month, the fetus is fully developed and could, if necessary, survive outside the womb. In the last two months, the fetus grows in size and puts on weight.

WALL OF UTERUS
INFERIOR VENA CAVA
AORTA
PSOAS MUSCLE
ILIAC CREST of PELVIS
ILIACUS MUSCLE
CHORION
UMBILICAL CORD
AMNION
PLACENTA
ABDOMINAL WALL
FATTY LAYER
BLADDER
PUBIC BONE
FATTY PAD
CLITORIS
URETHRA
CERVIX
VAGINA
RIGHT LEG
LEFT LEG

Squashed flat

Pregnancy brings enormous changes in the expectant mother's abdomen – turn to the previous spread and see the difference! The fetus takes up so much space that all the other organs are squashed flat. The mother may need to urinate more frequently because her bladder does not have as much room to expand, and eat smaller meals because her stomach is squashed.

Twist and turn

A fetus is active inside the uterus, changing its position, kicking its legs, and waving its arms around. The mother can feel these movements from the time the fetus is about four months old. The fetus also spends part of its day sleeping.

Exit from the womb

During pregnancy, the cervix, or neck of the womb, is tightly closed and plugged with mucus. As birth approaches, the muscles of the cervix relax and the mucus plug slips out, so that the fetus's head and body can pass through. Contractions of the muscles of the uterus push the fetus's head down as the cervix widens. The process of giving birth is such hard work that it is called "labor." When the baby is born, the umbilical cord is clamped and cut.

This ultrasound scan was made by a device that beams harmless high-pitched sound waves through the mother's abdomen, detects the echoes, and displays them on a computer screen. The scan shows a side view of the fetus, curled head-down, with the placenta to the left – as in the main picture. Scans such as these are usually done at 16-20 weeks of pregnancy, to check that the baby is healthy.

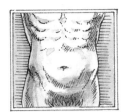

The Lower Back

SPRAINED JOINTS, strained muscles, and slipped disks – lower back problems seem to affect nearly everyone from time to time. This may be partly due to our upright posture, which is unique among our close relatives, the apes and monkeys (see below right). We keep our spines almost vertical as we walk and stand, which puts a great deal of strain on the lower back. This region must support the weight of the torso, head, neck, and arms. It is especially stressed when we lean forward, twist, or bend down to lift heavy objects.

Can you prevent back pain? Exercise and keep the muscles and joints shown here fit and healthy, so that they can better support and stabilize your lower spine. Good lifting technique also helps: Bend at the knees and hips while keeping your torso upright.

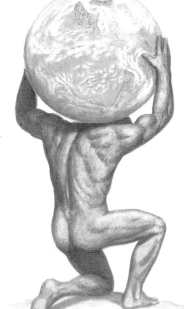

THE WEIGHT OF THE WORLD

In the mythical stories of the ancient Greeks, Atlas was one of the Titans, offspring of Uranus (god of Heaven) and Gaea (goddess of Earth). The Titans fought a war against the chief god, Zeus, and his Olympians, and lost. As a punishment, Atlas had to hold up the world forever. He is often pictured as a well-muscled man (left), the strength in his upper and lower back bearing the weight of the planet on his shoulders. The topmost bone of the spine, the atlas, is named after him because it supports the "globe" of the skull. Books of maps, such as this one, are also called atlases. This is because a collection of maps published in the 16th century featured a drawing of Atlas on its cover.

BAND OF BACK MUSCLES

Under the skin and the fatty layer just below it, the back is crisscrossed by broad bands of muscle. The muscles in your lower back provide support for your upright posture. The muscles at the top of the back move your shoulders and arms, and help you breathe. Those in the central group steady the spine and enable you to bend forward and back and twist to the side. Overlapping muscle sheets join this central region to the bony projections called flanges on the scapulae (shoulder blades) and pelvis (hips). Other muscles link these bones to the arms and legs.

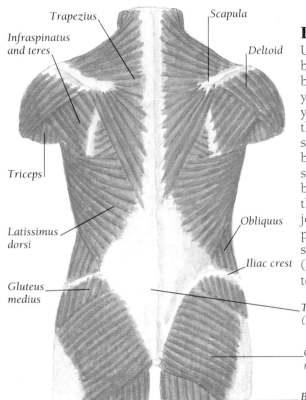

Trapezius
Infraspinatus and teres
Scapula
Deltoid
Triceps
Latissimus dorsi
Obliquus
Iliac crest
Gluteus medius
Thoracolumbar fascia (sheet of fibrous tissues)
Gluteus maximus
Biceps femoris and semitendinosus

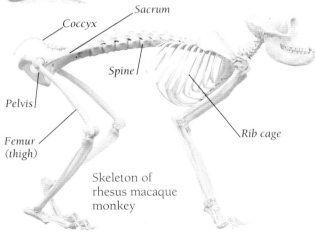

Coccyx
Sacrum
Spine
Pelvis
Femur (thigh)
Rib cage

Skeleton of rhesus macaque monkey

FOUR-LEGGED RELATIVE

This monkey, like most of our mammal relations, moves around on all fours. Its spine and thighs are approximately at right angles to each other. But this arrangement could not support a human's two-legged gait. During 5-10 million years of evolution, the human lower spine, hipbones, and hip joints have tilted so that the legs are directly beneath the main body, to support its balanced weight. This not only keeps us from toppling over, but also frees our arms and hands for grasping and manipulation.

THE PELVIC BONES

The bowl-shaped ring of bones at the base of the lower torso is called the pelvis (Latin for "basin"). It is formed by two innominate, or hip, bones at each side that curve around to meet at the pubic symphysis in the front, with the triangular base of the spine, the sacrum, between them in the back. Each hipbone consists of three individual bones that fuse during childhood: the flank bone, or ilium, the buttock bone, or ischium, and the pubic bone, or pubis. A woman's pelvis has a larger and more rounded hole in the center than a man's. This makes it easier for a baby to pass through this hole, known as the birth canal, as it leaves the uterus at birth.

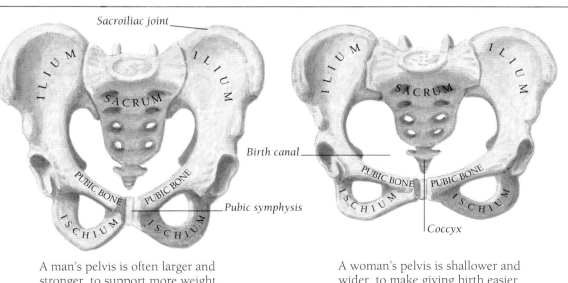

Sacroiliac joint
ILIUM
SACRUM
PUBIC BONE
ISCHIUM
Birth canal
Pubic symphysis
Coccyx

A man's pelvis is often larger and stronger, to support more weight.

A woman's pelvis is shallower and wider, to make giving birth easier.

AT THE BASE OF THE BACK

In this view of the lower torso from the rear, the main muscles and tough sheaths of fascia beneath the skin are shown on the right side. These are omitted from the left side, revealing the vertebrae of the spine with its network of spinal nerves and the hipbones joined to the sacrum at its base. The left kidney and the ureter can be seen resting against the rear surfaces of the intestines in front of them.

Around the back

The iliocostalis lumborum has several straps that link the lumbar vertebrae and sacrum with the lower six ribs. It is part of the long, complicated, muscle-and-tendon group, the erector spinae.

Bending over backward

The erector spinae groups run down each side of the spine, from the base of the skull to the hips and buttocks. The seven muscles in each group, including the longest, the longissimus thoracis, allow you to twist, lean, arch your back, and bend over backward.

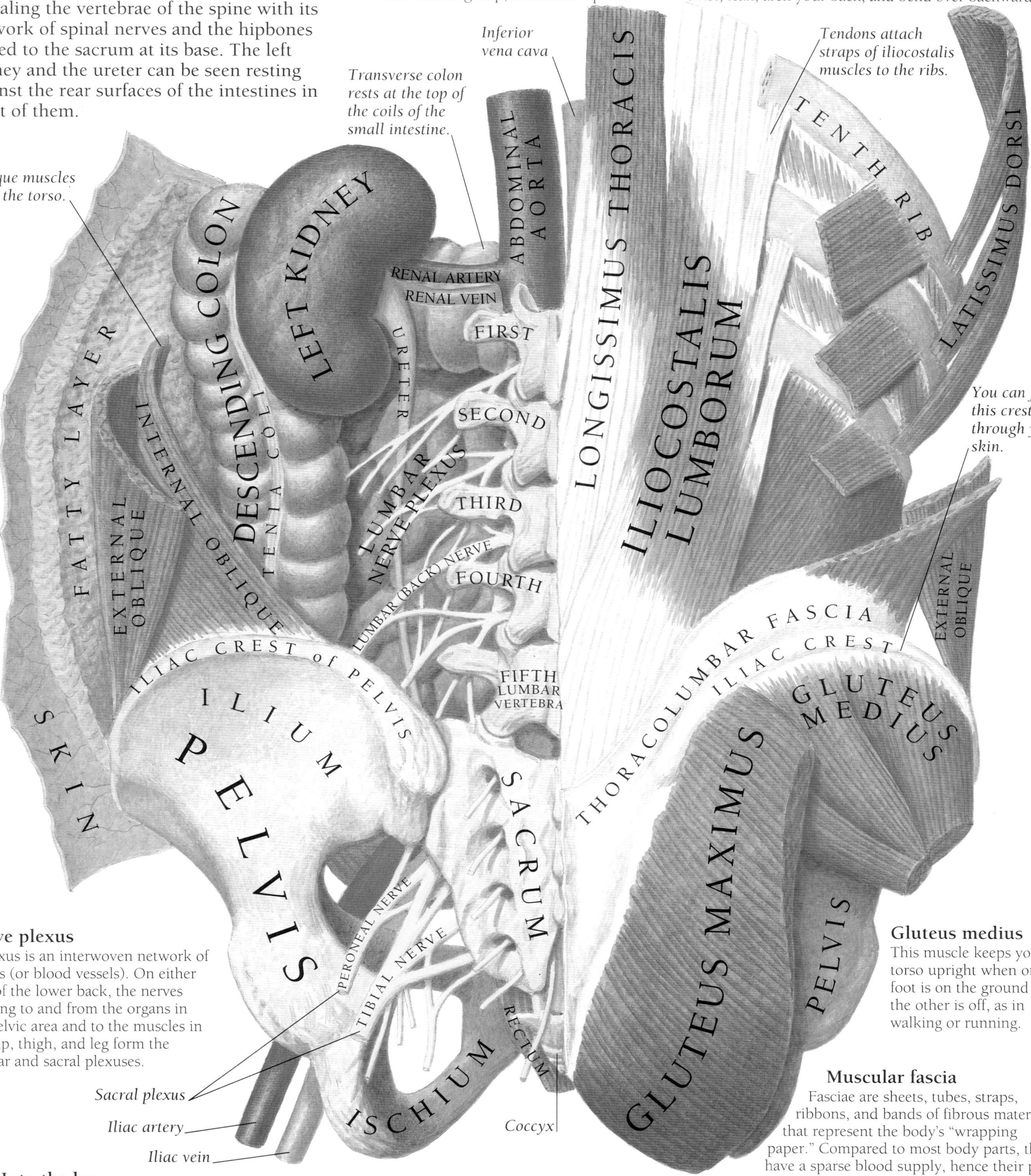

Oblique muscles twist the torso.

Transverse colon rests at the top of the coils of the small intestine.

Inferior vena cava

Tendons attach straps of iliocostalis muscles to the ribs.

You can feel this crest through your skin.

DESCENDING COLON

LEFT KIDNEY

ABDOMINAL AORTA

RENAL ARTERY
RENAL VEIN

FIRST

SECOND

THIRD

FOURTH

FIFTH LUMBAR VERTEBRA

LONGISSIMUS THORACIS

ILIOCOSTALIS LUMBORUM

TENTH RIB

LATISSIMUS DORSI

FATTY LAYER

EXTERNAL OBLIQUE

INTERNAL OBLIQUE

TENIA COLI

URETER

LUMBAR NERVE PLEXUS

LUMBAR (BACK) NERVE

ILIAC CREST of PELVIS

SKIN

ILIUM

PELVIS

SACRUM

ISCHIUM

THORACOLUMBAR FASCIA

ILIAC CREST

GLUTEUS MEDIUS

GLUTEUS MAXIMUS

PELVIS

EXTERNAL OBLIQUE

PERONEAL NERVE

TIBIAL NERVE

RECTUM

Coccyx

Nerve plexus

A plexus is an interwoven network of nerves (or blood vessels). On either side of the lower back, the nerves running to and from the organs in the pelvic area and to the muscles in the hip, thigh, and leg form the lumbar and sacral plexuses.

Sacral plexus

Iliac artery

Iliac vein

Into the leg

The pelvic area is one of the body's major junctions. Blood vessels, nerves, and lymph vessels branch out here to supply the structures within the abdomen. Then they divide to send branches into each leg. The iliac arteries are divisions of the abdominal aorta. The iliac veins meet to form the inferior vena cava.

Sacrum

The forces generated by your upper and lower body meet at the sacrum, th wedge of five fused bones that is the only connection between the spinal column and the pelvis.

Gluteus medius

This muscle keeps your torso upright when one foot is on the ground and the other is off, as in walking or running.

Muscular fascia

Fasciae are sheets, tubes, straps, ribbons, and bands of fibrous material that represent the body's "wrapping paper." Compared to most body parts, they have a sparse blood supply, hence their pale color. Fasciae cover many organs and pack the spaces between them. Some individual muscles and muscle groups are encased in fascial sheaths. These keep the muscles together and help anchor them to nearby bones, as in the thoracolumbar fascia above the crest of the pelvis.

The Leg and Foot

WALKING AND STANDING might seem easy, natural movements to you, but watch a year-old toddler totter with unsteady steps or sway and wobble while learning to stand. You soon realize what an effort these processes can be! Our two-legged gait is naturally unstable. Stand in one place for an hour or two, and your muscles begin to ache from the strain of the constant adjustments they make to keep your body balanced over your feet.

Before humans evolved to walk upright, arms and legs were very similar. The arrangements of bones and muscles is still much the same. The hip corresponds to the shoulder, and the knee to the elbow. But over millions of years, our legs have become adapted to carrying the weight of the body, while our arms are more suited to flexibility.

PEGLEG SAILOR

In days gone by, sailors risked "life and limb." Many an old seadog lost a leg – torn by the jaws of a shark, smashed by falling timbers, or caught in a last tightening rope. The leg contains no vital organs, but its powerful muscles receive a copious blood supply. So after the injury, the first priority would be to stanch the wound. As the stump healed, the next job would be to carve a replacement.

One famous "pegleg" was Captain Ahab, in Herman Melville's book Moby Dick.

Athletes jumping hurdles must swing two 22-pound (10-kg) weights – their legs – to and fro several times each second and lift them over the hurdles.

DOWN THE LEG

In this front view of the right leg, some of the muscles have been moved to reveal the various arteries, veins, and nerves snaking below and between them. In general, the front leg muscles straighten the knee, bend the ankle, and curl the toes. The muscles at the rear of the leg, shown below right, bend the knee and straighten the ankle.

Knee-kickers

Four large muscles cover the front and sides of the thigh. They are the rectus femoris (rectus means "straight") and the three-part vastus: the vastus lateralis, medialis, and intermedius. Together they make up the muscle group known as the quadriceps femoris, and they are used to straighten a bent knee, for example, when kicking a football.

A hinge for your leg

Your body's largest joint is the knee joint, located chiefly between the femur and tibia. It works like the hinge joint in your elbow, permitting you to fold your legs under when you kneel, or stretch them out to take a big step. It can swivel only slightly, helping you turn your foot to point your toes out or in.

The sartorius muscle has been cut away here to show the muscles in the front of the thigh.

The iliac artery branches out to carry fresh blood to the entire leg.

There are about 24 muscles in the hip and thigh region, which are used to swing the thigh to the side, back, and front.

Knees up

The gracilis brings the knee up and pulls it across the front, toward the middle of the body.

Longest muscle

The body's longest muscle is the sartorius. It runs, like a diagonal belt, down from the crest of the hipbone, across the front of the thigh, and along the inner side of the knee, where it is anchored on the upper end of the tibia. It helps bend both hip and knee, and twist the leg. This means you can stand on one leg and bend the other double, to look behind you at the sole of your other foot.

Wobbly knees

The patella, or kneecap, forms an odd sliding joint with the lower front of the femur. This disk-shaped bone rests on the shared tendon of the quadriceps femoris muscle group. If you sit on the floor with your leg stretched in front of you and relax your leg muscles, you can move the patella gently from side to side with your hand.

Illustration labels: ILIAC ARTERY · ILIACUS MUSCLE PSOAS · ILIUM · INGUINAL LIGAMENT · PUBIC BONE · TENSOR FASCIA LATA · SKIN OF THIGH · SARTORIUS · FEMORAL VEIN · FEMORAL ARTERY · GREAT SAPHENOUS VEIN · FEMORAL NERVE · GRACILIS · ADDUCTOR LONGUS · RECTUS FEMORIS · VASTUS LATERALIS · FATTY LAYER · VASTUS MEDIALIS · QUADRICEPS TENDON · PERONEAL NERVE · SKIN

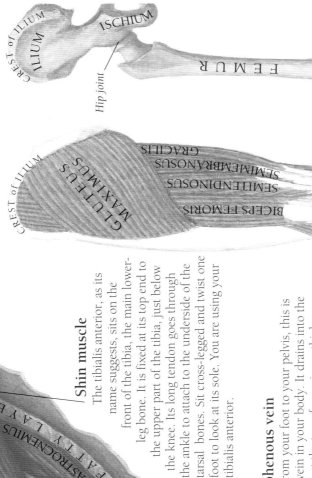

A REAR VIEW

Like the front of the leg, the rear is swathed in bulky muscles. They form bulges that can be felt through the layers of skin and fat. The main calf muscle, the gastrocnemius, has two major parts, or heads. Two common anatomical terms are used to name them: medial (toward the middle) and lateral (to the side). The medial head is nearer the middle of the body and the lateral head is on the outer side.

CREST of ILIUM
ILIUM
ISCHIUM
FEMUR
Hip joint
Knee joint
TIBIA
Popliteal (knee) fascia
Medial head
Fibula
Calcaneus (heel bone)

CREST of ILIUM
GLUTEUS MAXIMUS
BICEPS FEMORIS
SEMITENDINOSUS
SEMIMEMBRANOSUS
GRACILIS
GASTROCNEMIUS
GASTROCNEMIUS
ACHILLES TENDON
SOLEUS
Lateral head

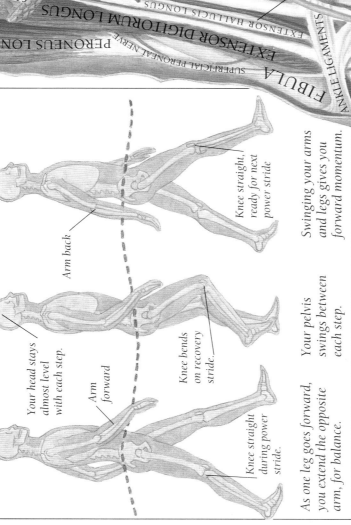

PATELLA
TIBIALIS ANTERIOR
TIBIA
PATELLAR LIGAMENT
LIGAMENT of SARTORIUS
GREAT SAPHENOUS VEIN
SOLEUS GASTROCNEMIUS
FATTY LAYER
TIBIALIS ANTERIOR
EXTENSOR DIGITORUM LONGUS
PERONEUS LONGUS
ANTERIOR TIBIAL VEIN & ARTERY
DEEP PERONEAL NERVE
SUPERFICIAL PERONEAL NERVE
FATTY LAYER
SAPHENOUS NERVE
GREAT SAPHENOUS VEIN
EXTENSOR HALLUCIS LONGUS
SUPERFICIAL PERONEAL NERVE
FIBULA
ANKLE LIGAMENTS
DORSAL VENOUS ARCH
FATTY PAD
FOOT
TENDONS of FOOT
EXTENSOR TENDON
HALLUX
DIGITS (TOES)

Shin muscle

The tibialis anterior, as its name suggests, sits on the front of the tibia, the main lower-leg bone. It is fixed at its top end to the upper part of the tibia, just below the knee. Its long tendon goes through the ankle to attach to the underside of the tarsal bones. Sit cross-legged and twist one foot to look at its sole. You are using your tibialis anterior.

Great saphenous vein

Stretching from your foot to your pelvis, this is the longest vein in your body. It drains into the femoral vein at the top of your inner thigh.

Shin extensors

The name "extensor" in the various front lower-leg muscles means that they extend (not flex) the parts below. That is, when you stand up, they pull the bones of your ankle and foot to raise your foot and toes.

Ankle joint

The ankle joint occurs where the lower ends of the tibia and the fibula slot neatly around the talus, the topmost of the seven tarsal bones in the foot. This hinged joint allows the foot to make up and down movements. Although individually the bones of the ankle and foot are delicate, they are bound together by strong ligaments and muscles.

The big toe, or hallux, has two bones, while the other toes have three.

THE MECHANICS OF WALKING

Walking has been called "controlled falling." You start by tipping your head and torso forward to the point of overbalance. Then you extend one leg to stop yourself from toppling over. Then you repeat the process. During the power stride, your body weight transfers from your heel to your toes as you push off and step ahead. Your pelvis tilts and the weight shifts to your other foot during the recovery stride.

As you step along, your leg muscles contract and relax in split-second unison. But the muscles in your torso, arms, neck, and head are hard at work, too. The main thrust for each step is provided by the muscles in the buttock and rear thigh, pulling your femur (thigh bone) down and back.

Knee straight, ready for next power stride.

Swinging your arms and legs gives you forward momentum.

Arm back

Your head stays almost level with each step.

Arm forward

Your pelvis swings between each step.

Knee bends on recovery stride.

As one leg goes forward, you extend the opposite arm, for balance.

Knee straight during power stride.

THE SPRING IN YOUR STEP

The foot lacks the delicate dexterity of the hand. Instead, it is a flexible platform whose elastic arched construction absorbs bumps and hollows in the ground as you walk and puts the spring in your step. The longest nerves in the body connect your toes with your brain far above.

The many nerve endings in your foot might make you ticklish there.

Toe bones

The bones of the digits, or toes, help you balance when standing and give the foot the grip and some of the strength to push off the ground when walking or running.

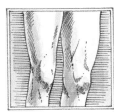

The Hip and Knee

Your hips and knees are the largest joints in your body. The hip joint is a ball-and-socket joint. The rounded head of your biggest bone, the femur, (thigh bone) fits snugly into a cup-shaped socket on your pelvis (hipbone). The hip is your leg's equivalent of your arm's shoulder. It is a much stronger joint than the shoulder, bound by tough ligaments and surrounded by your body's most powerful muscles. It is also more stable, to allow it to withstand the stresses of walking. What you gain in stability, however, you lose in mobility. You can swing your leg a fair way forward, less to the side, and only a little to the rear. Big movements, such as drawing your leg back, ready to kick, are possible only because the whole pelvis tilts over the other hip.

The knee joint works like a hinge to move your shin and foot forward and backward. Unlike the hinge joint in your elbow, it is a meeting of only two bones. Two knucklelike bumps on the lower end of the femur sit on twin dents in the upper part of the tibia.

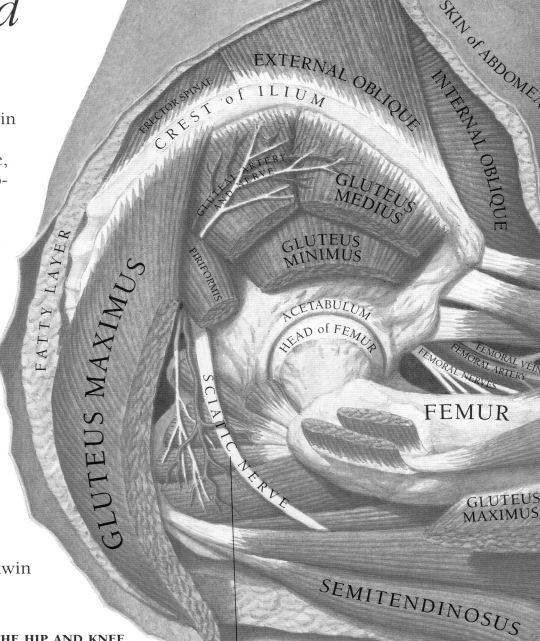

ERECTOR SPINAE
CREST of ILIUM
EXTERNAL OBLIQUE
SKIN of ABDOMEN
INTERNAL OBLIQUE
GLUTEAL ARTERY AND NERVE
GLUTEUS MEDIUS
GLUTEUS MINIMUS
PIRIFORMIS
FATTY LAYER
GLUTEUS MAXIMUS
ACETABULUM
HEAD of FEMUR
SCIATIC NERVE
FEMORAL VEIN
FEMORAL ARTERY
FEMORAL NERVES
FEMUR
GLUTEUS MAXIMUS
SEMITENDINOSUS

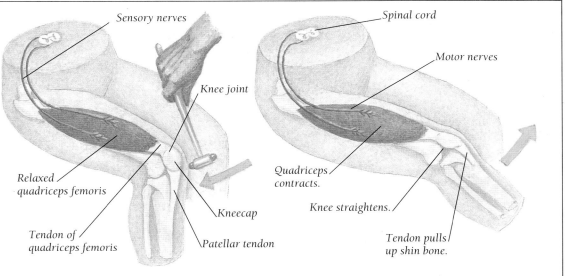

A skier bends the body at the knees, hips, and ankles, to stay stable and in control when skiing over bumps and hollows in the snow.

UNCOVERING THE HIP AND KNEE
The picture on the right delves deep into the leg, under the skin and many muscles, to uncover the details of the hip and knee joints. The socket of the pelvis, slightly smaller than your cupped hand, is at the junction of all three hipbones on each side, the ilium, ischium, and pubis. The femur in the thigh is your longest and strongest bone, representing about one-quarter of your total height.

Sciatic nerve
Stretching from the sacrum in the spine all the way down through the hamstring muscles in the thigh, this is the longest nerve in your body. The sciatic nerve carries messages to and from all of the muscles of the leg and foot, as well as supplying the back of the thigh. It divides into the common peroneal and tibial nerves.

FEEL A JERK
A reflex is an automatic reaction that your body does "on its own," without your brain thinking about it. You have dozens of reflexes, from blinking your eyelids shut when something gets too close to your eye, to sneezing when something gets up your nose. Doctors test your knee-jerk reflex to make sure your nerves are working well. A tap just below the kneecap stretches a tendon of the front thigh muscle. Sensors detect its movement and send nerve signals to the spinal cord. Reflex nerve connections in the cord send signals straight back out again, without "telling" your brain. These cause the thigh muscles to contract, jerking up your shin. This reflex may help you keep upright after a long time on your feet, when your knees may buckle.

Sensory nerves
Spinal cord
Knee joint
Motor nerves
Relaxed quadriceps femoris
Quadriceps contracts.
Kneecap
Knee straightens.
Tendon of quadriceps femoris
Patellar tendon
Tendon pulls up shin bone.

INSIDE THE KNEE

Extra ligaments and cartilage stabilize and support the knee joint and keep it from moving from side to side. The outside of the joint is bound with tough ligaments. Inside the joint are two short, stretchy ligaments, the cruciate ligaments, which join the femur to the tibia. In addition to the usual covering of cartilage on the ends of the bones, there are two crescent-shaped disks of cartilage called the menisci. These "float" in the knee joint and reduce friction between the moving bones.

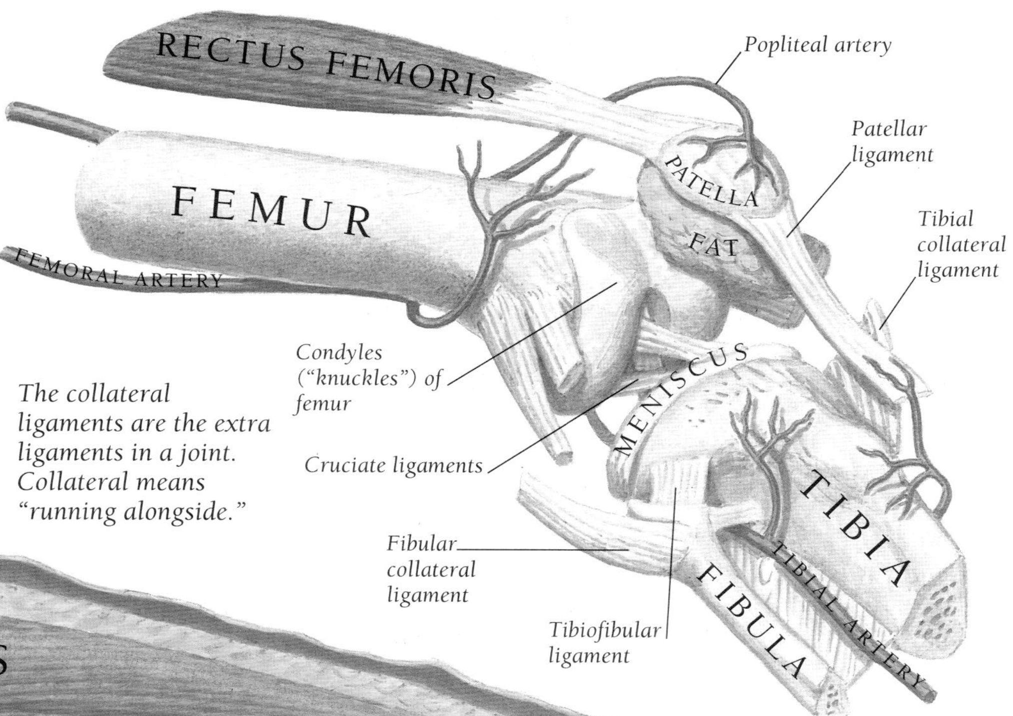

The collateral ligaments are the extra ligaments in a joint. Collateral means "running alongside."

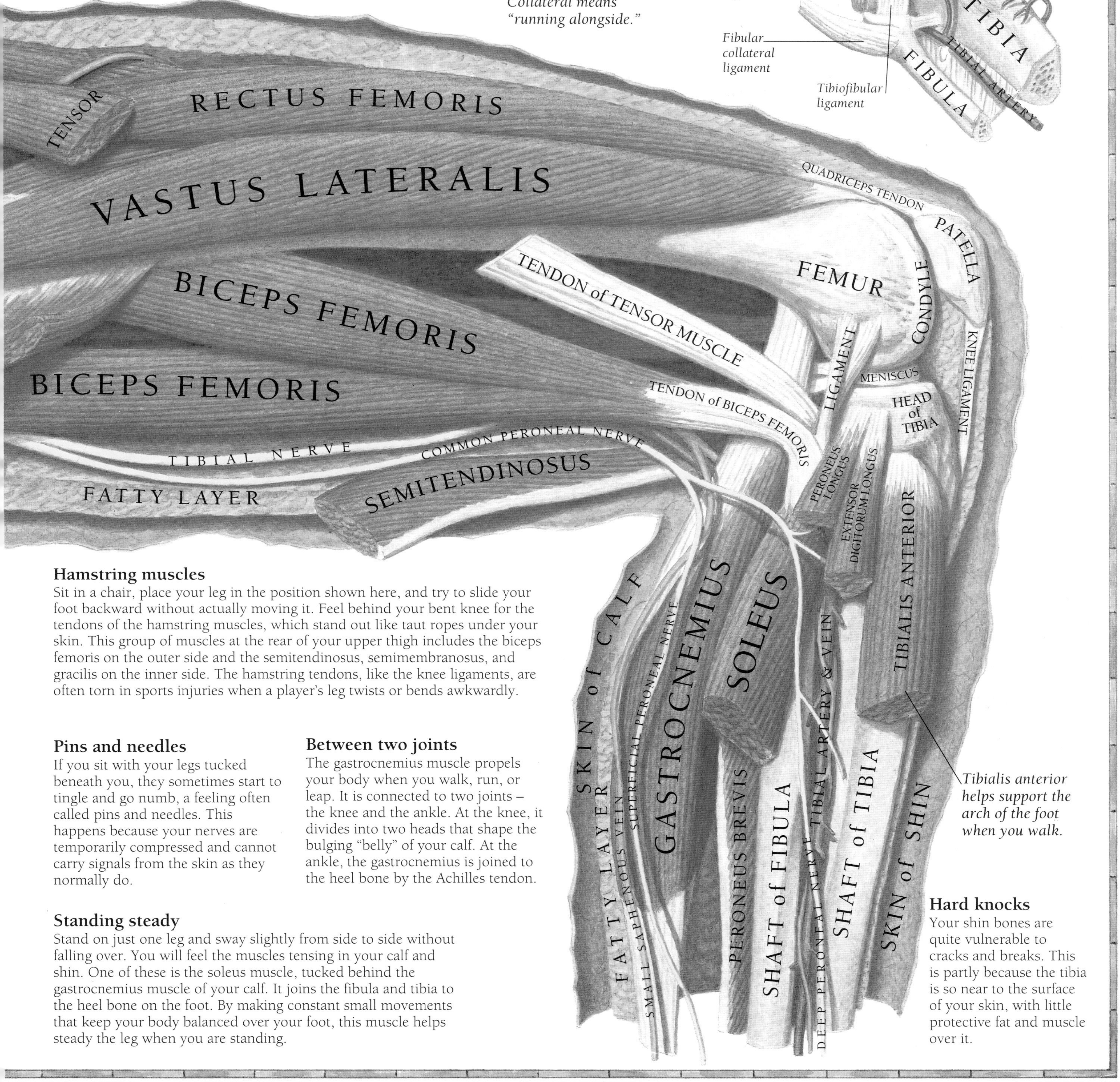

RECTUS FEMORIS

FEMUR

FEMORAL ARTERY

Popliteal artery

PATELLA

FAT

Patellar ligament

Tibial collateral ligament

Condyles ("knuckles") of femur

MENISCUS

Cruciate ligaments

TIBIA

Fibular collateral ligament

Tibiofibular ligament

TIBIAL ARTERY

FIBULA

TENSOR

RECTUS FEMORIS

VASTUS LATERALIS

BICEPS FEMORIS

BICEPS FEMORIS

TIBIAL NERVE

FATTY LAYER

COMMON PERONEAL NERVE

SEMITENDINOSUS

TENDON of TENSOR MUSCLE

QUADRICEPS TENDON

PATELLA

FEMUR

CONDYLE

KNEE LIGAMENT

MENISCUS

TENDON of BICEPS FEMORIS

LIGAMENT

HEAD of TIBIA

PERONEUS LONGUS

EXTENSOR DIGITORUM LONGUS

TIBIALIS ANTERIOR

SKIN of CALF

FATTY LAYER

SMALL SAPHENOUS VEIN

SUPERFICIAL PERONEAL NERVE

GASTROCNEMIUS

SOLEUS

PERONEUS BREVIS

SHAFT of FIBULA

DEEP PERONEAL NERVE

TIBIAL ARTERY & VEIN

SHAFT of TIBIA

SKIN of SHIN

Hamstring muscles

Sit in a chair, place your leg in the position shown here, and try to slide your foot backward without actually moving it. Feel behind your bent knee for the tendons of the hamstring muscles, which stand out like taut ropes under your skin. This group of muscles at the rear of your upper thigh includes the biceps femoris on the outer side and the semitendinosus, semimembranosus, and gracilis on the inner side. The hamstring tendons, like the knee ligaments, are often torn in sports injuries when a player's leg twists or bends awkwardly.

Pins and needles

If you sit with your legs tucked beneath you, they sometimes start to tingle and go numb, a feeling often called pins and needles. This happens because your nerves are temporarily compressed and cannot carry signals from the skin as they normally do.

Between two joints

The gastrocnemius muscle propels your body when you walk, run, or leap. It is connected to two joints – the knee and the ankle. At the knee, it divides into two heads that shape the bulging "belly" of your calf. At the ankle, the gastrocnemius is joined to the heel bone by the Achilles tendon.

Standing steady

Stand on just one leg and sway slightly from side to side without falling over. You will feel the muscles tensing in your calf and shin. One of these is the soleus muscle, tucked behind the gastrocnemius muscle of your calf. It joins the fibula and tibia to the heel bone on the foot. By making constant small movements that keep your body balanced over your foot, this muscle helps steady the leg when you are standing.

Tibialis anterior helps support the arch of the foot when you walk.

Hard knocks

Your shin bones are quite vulnerable to cracks and breaks. This is partly because the tibia is so near to the surface of your skin, with little protective fat and muscle over it.

The Ankle and Foot

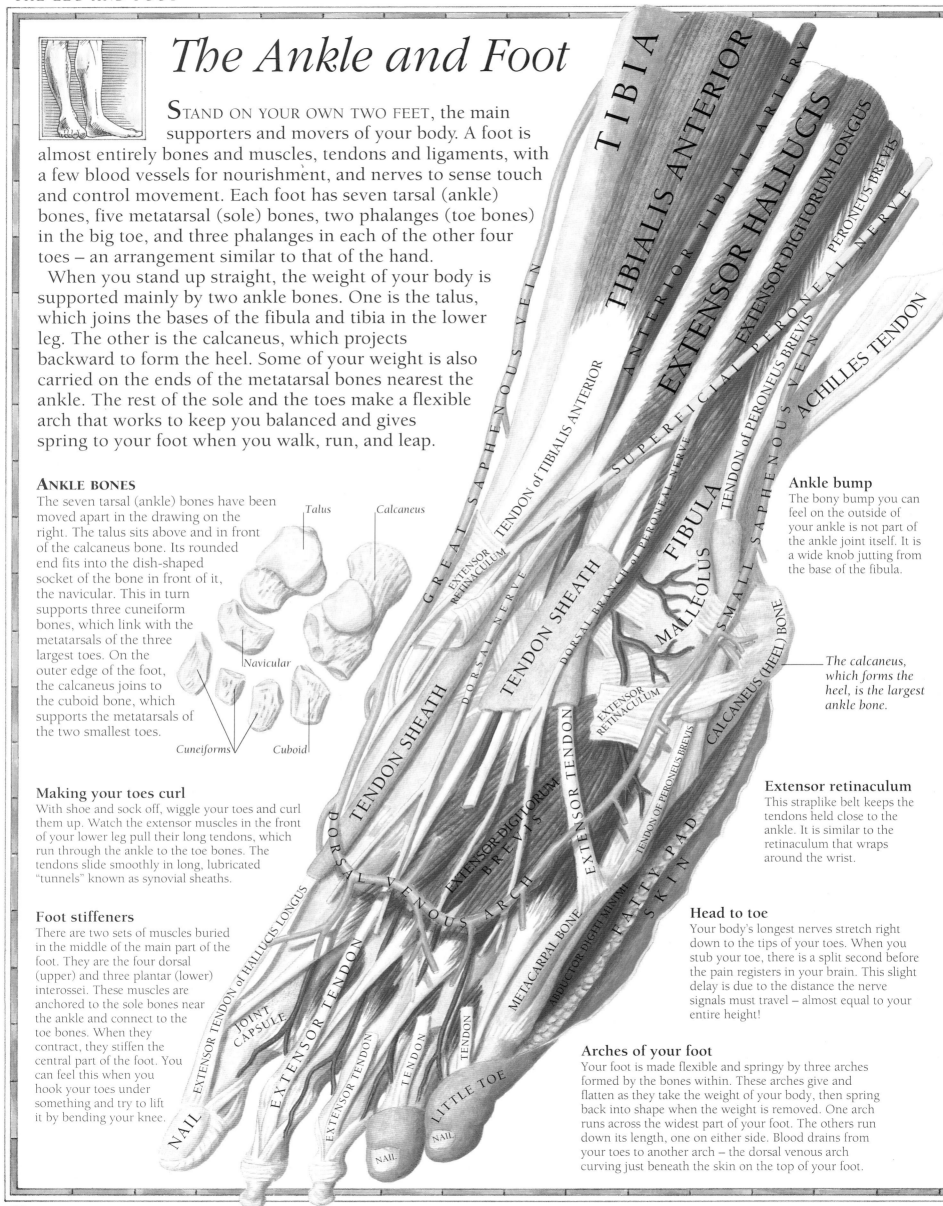

Stand on your own two feet, the main supporters and movers of your body. A foot is almost entirely bones and muscles, tendons and ligaments, with a few blood vessels for nourishment, and nerves to sense touch and control movement. Each foot has seven tarsal (ankle) bones, five metatarsal (sole) bones, two phalanges (toe bones) in the big toe, and three phalanges in each of the other four toes – an arrangement similar to that of the hand.

When you stand up straight, the weight of your body is supported mainly by two ankle bones. One is the talus, which joins the bases of the fibula and tibia in the lower leg. The other is the calcaneus, which projects backward to form the heel. Some of your weight is also carried on the ends of the metatarsal bones nearest the ankle. The rest of the sole and the toes make a flexible arch that works to keep you balanced and gives spring to your foot when you walk, run, and leap.

ANKLE BONES

The seven tarsal (ankle) bones have been moved apart in the drawing on the right. The talus sits above and in front of the calcaneus bone. Its rounded end fits into the dish-shaped socket of the bone in front of it, the navicular. This in turn supports three cuneiform bones, which link with the metatarsals of the three largest toes. On the outer edge of the foot, the calcaneus joins to the cuboid bone, which supports the metatarsals of the two smallest toes.

Making your toes curl

With shoe and sock off, wiggle your toes and curl them up. Watch the extensor muscles in the front of your lower leg pull their long tendons, which run through the ankle to the toe bones. The tendons slide smoothly in long, lubricated "tunnels" known as synovial sheaths.

Foot stiffeners

There are two sets of muscles buried in the middle of the main part of the foot. They are the four dorsal (upper) and three plantar (lower) interossei. These muscles are anchored to the sole bones near the ankle and connect to the toe bones. When they contract, they stiffen the central part of the foot. You can feel this when you hook your toes under something and try to lift it by bending your knee.

Ankle bump

The bony bump you can feel on the outside of your ankle is not part of the ankle joint itself. It is a wide knob jutting from the base of the fibula.

The calcaneus, which forms the heel, is the largest ankle bone.

Extensor retinaculum

This straplike belt keeps the tendons held close to the ankle. It is similar to the retinaculum that wraps around the wrist.

Head to toe

Your body's longest nerves stretch right down to the tips of your toes. When you stub your toe, there is a split second before the pain registers in your brain. This slight delay is due to the distance the nerve signals must travel – almost equal to your entire height!

Arches of your foot

Your foot is made flexible and springy by three arches formed by the bones within. These arches give and flatten as they take the weight of your body, then spring back into shape when the weight is removed. One arch runs across the widest part of your foot. The others run down its length, one on either side. Blood drains from your toes to another arch – the dorsal venous arch curving just beneath the skin on the top of your foot.

LITTLE TOE

FLEXOR TENDON

FOURTH LUMBRICAL

FLEXOR TENDON

THIRD LUMBRICAL

FLEXOR TENDON

SECOND LUMBRICAL

FLEXOR TENDON

FIRST LUMBRICAL

FLEXOR TENDON of HALLUCIS LONGUS

FLEXOR HALLUCIS BREVIS

ABDUCTOR TENDON

PLANTAR APONEUROSIS

ABDUCTOR DIGITI MINIMI

FLEXOR DIGITI MINIMI

FLEXOR DIGITORUM BREVIS

PLANTAR APONEUROSIS

ABDUCTOR HALLUCIS

FATTY PAD of SOLE

CALCANEUS (HEEL) BONE

Flexor muscles arch the foot and pull the toes down.

The abductor hallucis muscle's primary purpose is to flex the big toe.

ACHILLES TENDON (CALCANEUS TENDON)

At 6 in. (15 cm) long, the Achilles tendon is the longest tendon in your body – and the strongest.

Calcaneus tendon
The calcaneus tendon, linking the gastrocnemius and soleus muscles in the calf to the calcaneus bone, is also called the Achilles tendon. Achilles was a hero in Greek mythology. When he was a child, his mother tried to make him invincible by dipping him in the waters of the River Styx. Because she held him by his heel, it never touched the water, making this his one weak spot. Achilles was later killed in a battle when an arrow pierced his heel.

The fibers of a tendon, shown in this photomicrograph, are embedded in the outer surface of the bone.

THE BASE OF THE BODY
The sole of your foot bears your entire body weight when you stand still and withstands a force equivalent to up to five times your body weight when you are on the move. Tough straps and bands of dense, fibrous tissue, such as the plantar aponeurosis, secure the muscles and tendons that move the bones. The skin of the sole can be more than 0.2 inch (0.5 mm) thick, the thickest in the body. Toes – like fingers – have ridged prints.

Sole of your foot
Just under the skin and fat is the plantar aponeurosis, a dense network of crisscrossing collagen fibers that forms a secure base for the foot, like the inner sole of a shoe.

Fiber and fat
The thick pads of fat in the soles have stringy fibers growing through and between them. This design works in the same way that the crisscrossed stitching in a quilt stops the filling from bunching up around the edges. It prevents the shock-cushioning fat from being squeezed out to the sides of the foot.

Sole muscles
The main actions of the sole (plantar) muscles are to arch the whole foot and to curl the toes downward. You use these muscles when you curl your toes around the edge of a swimming pool, before diving in. The most powerful ones pull on the bones of the big toe, or hallux.

HANDS AND FEET
The bones in your hands and feet share not only the same names, but also the same arrangement, as shown in these skeletal views. The hand bones are thinner and lighter and their joints are more flexible. The foot is designed for weightbearing, although with practice, people unable to use their hands have learned to write, type, and paint with their toes.

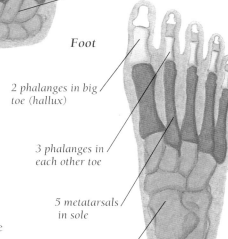

Hand
- 3 phalanges in each finger
- 2 phalanges in thumb
- 5 metacarpals in palm
- 8 carpals in wrist

Foot
- 2 phalanges in big toe (hallux)
- 3 phalanges in each other toe
- 5 metatarsals in sole
- 7 tarsals in ankle

GETTING OFF ON THE RIGHT FOOT
No other mammal, and few other animals, can walk with our smooth, two-legged stride. The leg acts as a system of levers. The calcaneus bone of your heel sticks out to the rear of the joint between the shinbones and the ankle. When you take a step, it touches the ground first. Then the calf muscles contract, pulling the heel up. Forward push is provided by the ball of your foot. As your entire body weight shifts to the bones in the front of your foot, its arch shape flattens so that the weight is evenly distributed. One final push is provided by the flexor muscles of your big toe. The front shin muscles lift up the front of the foot, and you are ready to take another step.

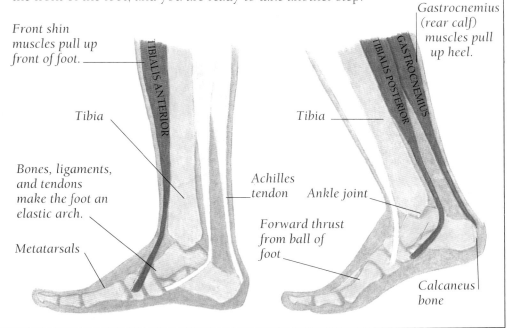

Front shin muscles pull up front of foot.

TIBIALIS ANTERIOR

Tibia

Bones, ligaments, and tendons make the foot an elastic arch.

Metatarsals

Gastrocnemius (rear calf) muscles pull up heel.

GASTROCNEMIUS

TIBIALIS POSTERIOR

Tibia

Achilles tendon

Ankle joint

Forward thrust from ball of foot

Calcaneus bone

Index

Acknowledgments

Dorling Kindersley thanks Shelagh Gibson for
production, Anna Kunst for translation,
Ann Kramer and Miranda Smith for editorial
assistance, and Lynn Bresler for the index.

Additional illustrations Susanna Addario,
Jon Rogers, and John Hutchinson

Picture credits

(b = bottom, c = center, l = left, r = right, t = top)
Colorsport 2bl, 24 tr, 36 cl, 58 cl. Mary Evans
Picture Library 34tr, 47br, 58br. Robert Harding
Picture Library 32tl. Image Bank/G.K. & Vikki
Hart 60cl. Mansell Collection 38tc. National
Medical Slide Bank 16bl. Ann Ronan 18cl.
Science Photo Library 14bl/Dr Tony Brain 17tr;

Dr Goron Bredberg 19cr; CNRI 3tl, 3tr, 4bl,
4bc, 6cl, 10bl, 10br, 27tr, 30cl, 45tr, 48tr, 51t,
55br; CNRI/Secchi-Lecaque-Roussel-UCLAF
46bl; D. Fawcett & D. Phillips 8tr; Simon
Fraser 3tcl, 22cl; Bruce Inverson 31br;
Manfred Kage 7tr, 16 cl, 40tr; Dr Mertyn
Gorman 24cl; Astrid & Hans-Frider Michler

63bl; Hank Morgan 38cl; Professors P.M.
Motta & J. van Blerkom 3tcr, 52bl; Motta
& Familari, Anatomy Dept, University La
Sapienza, Rome 54cl; Alfred Pasieks 39cr;
Dr Klaus Schiller 43tc, 43tr. Zefa 50cl.

Picture research Catherine O'Rourke